Massimiliano Angelucci

SPORTS AND MYSTIFICATION

Biblioteca Italiana
Italienische Bibliothek  Frankfurt am Main

Biblioteca Italiana / Italienische Bibliothek
Frankfurt am Main

Massimiliano Angelucci, 1975.
Sports and Mystification.
Translated from the Italian by Isabella Cultrera.
Edited by Sylver Foley.
Proofread by Lana Ljustina.

Book design by Massimiliano Angelucci

First published in Italy in 2016 by Robin Edizioni under title: *Sport e mistificazione.*

ISBN 978-3-9817586-2-7

For Lana

This is not an objective book
There is a preconceived idea, a choice of subject
It is written taking the side of men

Raniero La Valle

CONTENTS

Introduction 1

Sports and militarism 9

Sports and nationalism.. 15

Sports and olympism.. 21

Sports and religion... 41

Sports and work... 47

Sports and entertainment... 55

Sports and power... 63

Sports and capitalism 71

Sports and industrialism... 77

Sports and record... 83

Sports and doping.. 89

Sports and alienation 97

Sports and education.. 101

Sports and detriment.. 105

Sports and pacifism 113

Sports and benefit.. 121

Conclusions 127

Bibliography 133

Introduction

Mystification, an eighteenth century French word deriving from the Greek "μύστης", indicates a deliberate distortion of truth and reality, as well as an abuse of the credulity of others by spreading incorrect information.[1]

Small, although certainly insidious examples, can be found everywhere in the lexical manipulation that is typical of the political and commercial contemporary language. Just think about an oxymoron like "good war", "sustainable development" or "religious sciences", invented to soften and essentially distort the original meaning.

Among the most ancient and effective prototypes of mystification, enough to influence human history, was the so-called "Donation of Constantine" *(Constitutum Constantini)*, the false decree which insisted on dating back to the year 313 and with which the emperor - miraculously healed of leprosy thanks to a christening - would have converted to Christianity and would have given the Catholic Church a number of goods, privileges, the dominion over the Roman Empire of the West and the superiority of papal power over the imperial itself. This also gave the pontiffs a pretext for subsequent claims, which happened several times over the centuries and even after the philologist Lorenzo Valla, in 1440, managed to irrefutably expose and prove the apocryphal nature of the document.

The multifaceted phenomenon hidden behind the word "sport" skillfully eludes the many attempts to define it, to the extent that one of the sharpest definitions could be: «Sports are what people do when thinking they are playing sports».[2] However, it is possible to identify the etymological path and key components that are common to the most authoritative sources. The origin of the word from the Latin *"dēporto"*, to indicate the occasional outing outside the city walls to engage in leisure activities and the transition to the Old French *"desport"* (XII-XIII century) with a meaning not very different from fun, which remains essentially unchanged both in the English *"disport"* of the XIV century and in its definitive abbreviation into *"sport"* which took place in the XVI century. It then identifies a free and unproductive activity, characterized by a predominant motor component, possible forms of regulation and practiced for recreation, leisure and well-being.

Sports have been since ancient times - when such term did not even exist - a "total social fact", meaning capable, as theorized by Mauss, to influence other areas of society. Now more than ever, sports are ubiquitous, so much that everyone believes they know everything about them. Just like it happens with meteorology, everyone constantly talks about it, expresses opinions, and quotes proverbs, common places and forecasts without having actual knowledge or having ever studied the subject.

The complexity of the phenomenon makes the breakdown in all its parts (or matrices), which have become stratified and overlapped over time, necessary for a greater understanding:[3]

First of all the "military" one, most ancient of all, lacks the recreational aspect and calls for the fortification of the body aimed at war.

The "health" matrix, almost as ancient as the previous one, was able to progressively acquire more credibility and authority with the increasing discoveries in the anatomical and physiological areas. It relies on the correct intuition that one's health can be restored, preserved and enhanced through a correctly dosed movement.

The "educational" matrix, also called pedagogical, was born in the fifteenth century and it supports the skills of the physical exercise not in terms of health benefits, but also to shape the individual.

The "competitive" matrix interprets the recreational movement as opposed to other individuals or groups.

The "aesthetic" matrix, the result of social transformations that have led to the development of the current aesthetic model which tends to be a slim and toned figure, sets the body movement, carried out in various forms, as a means for an improvement mostly in such direction.

The "representative" matrix describes the transformation of sports as expedient for a profession which leads to the identification of these moments as "sports representations", equivalent and indistinguishable from other television or theatrical performances (in which the athlete is then the equivalent of the show's actor/man).

The "projective" matrix includes the enormous offer of passive use (without movement) through the various media, which resulted in the birth of a new category of "sportsmen"; that big share of fans whose relationship with sports is sometimes very intense, but which is established exclusively, or almost, in passive mode, following the various disciplines through the mass media. These sports are the manifest expression of a mechanism (projective, precisely) that allows them each time to identify themselves in the athlete or teams followed, and therefore to "practice" sports outside of their own body.

The "expressive" matrix represents human movement arising from the need to express their individuality. It includes the activity often not organized, carried out in solitary and shared only in sporadic occasions, like so-called "extreme" sports and some dance types.

The "virtual" matrix, lastly, includes sports practices simulated through technological devices, capable of involving not only the fingers like in the earliest types of video games, but through the use of the entire body, or almost.

Among all these - as you will see - one has prevailed, which is the sum of the deteriorating forms; military, competitive, representative and projective.

From a chronological point of view, in different periods of human history these motor practices have mirrored and supported the needs of the time. There are signs of those that can be traced back to gaming activities or utilities (medical gymnastics, fencing with sticks, fight, dances and marches) already in Crete in 3000 BCE but of course the Sumerians, Assyrians, Babylonians, Hittites, Phoenicians, Egyptians, Greeks, Etruscans and Romans also had them.

The "unproductive" game is common to all eras and was accompanied in different periods and places by other practices. The need for food (hunting and fishing) led to finding exercises aimed at developing skills that could be useful for such purposes. This is why new tool inventions came to the rescue, like arrowheads (origin of archery) and spears (javelin). Likewise, the need to move around from one place to another via land, water, ice and air, gave life to disciplines and multiple expertise within them; running by foot, horseback riding (horseracing) or running via mechanical means (cycling and other transportation on wheels, like motorcycles, motor racings), swimming and various forms of navigation, like locomotion and skating on ice with special footwear, skates or means pulled by animals, up to flying (parachuting and other simple or motorized mechanical means).

The medieval practices distinguished themselves from those aimed at the exercise of the working skills, however marginal, and those distinctly related to the war (tournaments, carousels and knights exercises in general) united by the use of weapons. These witnessed, in time, a progressive slackening of the cruel component in favor of an increasing regulation.[4]

Modern sports were born during the eighteenth century in England, which was undergoing industrialization, and then they spread to the United States, to Western Europe and other parts of the world, primarily through trade connections.[5]

In the vision of the founder of the International Olympic Committee, sports are «the voluntary and habitual cult of the intensive muscular effort based on the desire for progress and which can even be risky. Exercise must be practiced with ardor, I would even say with violence. Sports are not the physical exercise suitable for all, provided that you have to be wise and moderate; sports are the pleasure of the strong, or those who wish to become it».[6]

With a definition devoid of many superhuman connotations, the European Union instead defines sports as «All forms of physical activity which, through casual or organised participation, aim at expressing or improving physical fitness and mental well-being and forming social relationships, or obtaining results in competition at all levels».[7]

However, in reality, between an organized or not organized participation - and between professionalism and amateurism - the first ones have prevailed without leaving room for a spontaneous and carefree practice, just like the expression of a goal or improvement of a physical and mental condition, which end up suffering even negative effects. What remains is clearly the "…obtainment of results in competition at all levels".

The study of sports finds more shadows than lights, and raises more doubts than certainties; board games that are exclusively of thought like checkers, chess or bridge, for example, are recognized by the Olympic committee as sports despite having a motor component equal to the reading of this book. On the contrary, playing musical instruments like a piano, although it requires great coordination, substantial capacity and motor skills, as well as a constant "training", has never been linked to the sports world. This exemplifies the enormous importance linked by the hegemonic conception of sports to just competitive aspect, clearly the only real discriminant taken into consideration.

This and many other signs of a highly ideologized sports disguised with fake correctness and false philanthropy are highlighted in the following pages, through a series of more or less synthetic points. In most of them, very specific references are deliberately avoided, in order to not to give the impression that it is only a few isolated cases. The problem today, in fact, is not so much the lack of information, which is available in many forms and sources if one just looks hard enough, but, if anything, an insidious overload of information, most of which is misleading or about trivial issues, so that it constitutes a permanent "background noise" under which even those that should receive attention are inevitably likely to remain submerged.

It is said that writing is the guardian of the word and therefore of the human knowledge. It is entrusted, in this case, with a renovated critique theory that - wrote Horkheimer - has the task of expressing that which is generally concealed. The masses, in fact, end up not realizing when these changes take place, especially when they occur gradually, and they tend to believe what they are repeatedly told and to behave in a uniform way, even towards wrong choices.

NOTES

[1] ISTITUTO DELLA ENCICLOPEDIA ITALIANA e CENTRE NATIONAL DE RESSOURCES TEXTUELLES ET LEXICALES.

[2] PAUL IRLINGER, CATHERINE LOUVEAU e MICHÈLE MÉTOUDI, *Les pratiques sportives des Français* (Paris: INSEP, 1987), 15.

[3] MASSIMILIANO ANGELUCCI, *La Responsabilità Sociale nello Sport* (Roma: Aracne, 2009).

[4] ALLEN GUTTMANN, *Dal rituale al record. La natura degli sport moderni* (Napoli: Edizioni Scientifiche Italiane, 1994), 80. Orig. *From Ritual to Record: The Nature of Modern Sports* (New York: Columbia University Press, 1978).

[5] *Ibidem*, 79.

[6] PIERRE DE FRÉDY DE COUBERTIN, *Pédagogie sportive* (Paris: Crés, 1922).

[7] COUNCIL OF EUROPE, *European Sport Charter* (Ródos: Council of Europe, 1992).

Sports and militarism

1. Modern sports are the continuation of politics and war through other means.[1] It is the institutional symbolization[2] and the war, as comparison between nations which aim to prevail and arrive "first",[3] with all its components that are common to today's sports, can be considered the bloodiest of them all.
2. Supremacy and domination, personal and territorial, are the purposes of mystified sports.
3. The opposition that characterizes sports is based on a dispute and confrontation that was originally just interpersonal, then became between groups and ultimately between cliques and classes. The organization into families, tribes and various groups originally had the aim of safeguarding the availability of certain individual or collective privileges. These structures have been later on replaced by specialized groups and appointed specifically to the role of defenders such as the army and, in sports, the teams that "defend", in fact, the colors of neighborhoods, cities, nations, or other groups.[4]
4. The army of ancient Rome, in order to achieve a more agile maneuver overcame the concept of compact phalanx and introduced very strict battle positions, mainly on four levels (*velites, hastati, principes* and *triarii*). The same is evident in the tactical modules of team sports.[5]
5. The modern "territorial" sports type perfectly evoke the symbolisms of war or, according to the zoologist and ethologist Desmond John Morris,[6] of ritual hunting, with the defense and conquest. Among the most common, soccer and rugby are derived from different regulations of violent practices then defined with the name of medieval soccer. These saw groups of nearby countries confront each other in the countryside with the purpose of reaching the symbolic conquest of the rival with a sphere of animal gut. In modern times, the points clearly express the unit of measure of the violation on the enemy (prey) or on its territory variously represented by doors and boundaries of the field of action.
6. The training and preparatory function of the military activity of many sports is still evident today.

7. Just like in the military field, the concepts of obedience and respect for the hierarchy are essential in modern sports. The sense of individual responsibility of the person dangerously fades away just like in war, where the justification for which we merely follow orders is common.[7] The discipline thus obtained is even more effective since it is self-imposed.

8. Modern sports are born with a strong nationalistic or patriotic-military connotation.[8]

9. Sports clubs in several countries, especially those in Eastern Europe, are the expression of national armies (such as the Partizan Belgrade and Steaua București) or they even still bear their names (like in the case of CSKA Moskva, where the acronym stands for "central sports club army"). In England, there is the "Arsenal", founded in an explosives factory and therefore symbolized by a war cannon, which is why fans and soccer players are called "gunners".

10. Modern sports have spread due to military and commercial occupations and colonization, according to imperialist schemes. Thus we find very different and distant countries that end up having the same "national" sports, just think of England and India. In other cases, like with exotic motor races that have the heroic charm of the "domestication of the far away land",[9] sports colonialism is purely suffered and not even practiced in the hosting territories.

11. As noted by Hoberman,[10] the rhythmic mass choreographies typical of the sports conception in the totalitarian regimes, with thousands of gymnasts in the stadium who perform coordinated movements while marching, saluting and singing in unison, essentially represent the ceremony of the garrison state.

12. The sports and military ceremonials are so similar that, on many occasions, they coincide.[11]

13. Even countries where the approach to sports was fundamentally anti-competitive, such as Russia and China, are turning to a highly competitive doctrine. In this regard, one of the most controversial presidents of the Olympic Committee said in 1955 that Russia was building the biggest mass army of athletes the world has ever known.[12]

14. The bond between the Olympic committees and military field is also confirmed by the fact that some of these, like the Italian

National Olympic Committee, for example, were founded by members of the army. In many countries, athletes with good qualities in Olympic disciplines are recruited in the army and paid to take part in military sports. These State athletes are therefore real "sport soldiers" who are sent on missions abroad at every international event.

15. Modern sports makes heavy use of symbols. The official badges and names of sports organizations besides representing territorial places recall, and in some cases coincide with the military ones. At least, they have the same aggressive symbolism used by the military, like the abused reference to fierce animals.

16. Sportswear is the perfect transposition of military uniforms in sports. Combined with the use of standards, flags and banners, it is essential to strengthen the feeling of identity and to distinguish "us" from "them", the adversary, the enemy to be fought. In team sports, hierarchies are manifested through a different band, or a uniform proudly worn by an athlete called "captain".

17. The aggressive instinctive background and the affinity with the military terminology - Vinnai highlights in his book about football and ideologies [13] - clearly appear also in soccer language. The opponent is "beat", "run over", "neutralized", "wiped out", "annihilated", "rendered harmless", "besieged", "appalled" or "dismissed". A successful player is designated as "gunner", "bomber", "battering ram" or "destroyer". He is defined as a "fighter", "clever", "killer", "explosive", "incisive", "hard", "cold" or "ruthless". Again, the shots at the goal are defined as "missiles", "bombs", "rockets", "cannon shots", "gunshots", "lashes" or "hits".[14] Even the military terms "tournament" (which defines the fight of armed knights in medieval times) and "maneuver" are still commonly used in sports.

18. It may also happen, like in July 1969, that the symbolic war of the sports and the real one will occur the same time and place, in what went down in history as the "War of the *Fútbol*" fought between the states of Honduras and El Salvador. The thousands of deaths and wounded made it one of the bloodiest battles of the Second World War.

19. In sports language it is said that "the flags (other military reference) no longer exist", proving that, just like the mercenaries, sportsmen are sold and "fight" on the side of the highest bidder.

20. The other fighters, the hordes of fans, with their aggressive and often violent behavior, their hierarchies, their tribal relations systems, their concept of "honor" and "barrack" rules, remarkably remind of the forms of paramilitary groups.

21. At the time of the disintegration of Yugoslavia, nationalist militias were recruited precisely among the organized groups of supporters and specifically these, on May 13, 1990 at the Maksimir stadium in Zagreb, triggered the conflict that gave spark to the Croatian War of Independence. Even today, a monument located outside the stadium quotes: «To all the supporters of Dinamo, for whom the war began on 13-V-1990 in Maksimir stadium and who left their lives on the altar of their homeland Croatia».

22. Sports medicine itself has a similar military method and the common purpose of ensuring the most rapid and complete functional recovery of the wounded/injured players in order to be able to send them back as soon as possible in the battle/game. During the Second World War experiments on doping, a typical sports phenomenon, were practiced on the soldiers.[15]

23. Modern sports are a constant expression of a militarized society.[16]

24. The sports mystification constantly evokes an irritating "heroism without purpose" [17] and the sportsmen are hence heroes of "imagined communities"[18] rather than real ones.

NOTES

[1] Paraphrase the famous saying of CARL PHILIPP GOTTLIEB VON CLAUSEWITZ, *Vom Kriege: Hinterlassenes Werk des Generals Carl von Clausewitz* (Berlin: Dümmler, 1832).

[2] JEAN-MARIE BROHM, *Sociologie politique du sport* (Nancy: Presses Universitaires de Nancy, 1992), 315. Orig. Paris: Éditions Universitaires, 1976.

[3] Georges Hébert in JEAN-MARIE BROHM, *Ibidem*, 23.

[4] Alfredo Calligaris in GIUSEPPE BRUNAMONTINI, *Esercito e Sport. Dal gesto individuale del guerriero mitologico all'educazione sportiva dei giovani di oggi* (Bari: Laterza, 1989), 167.

[5] *Ibidem*, 162.

[6] DESMOND JOHN MORRIS, *The Soccer Tribe* (London: Jonathan Cape, 1981).

[7] JOE HUMPHREYS, *Foul Play: What's wrong with Sport* (London: Icon Books, 2008), 52.

[8] Fausto Colombo in GIUSEPPE BRUNAMONTINI, op. cit., 74.

[9] GEORGES VIGARELLO, *Culture e tecniche dello sport. Gesti, strumenti, materiali, organizzazioni: un'antropologia dei fenomeni sportivi nella società contemporanea* (Milano: il Saggiatore, 1993), 168. Orig. *Une histoire culturelle du sport*. Paris: Éditions Robert Laffont, 1988.

[10] *Ibidem*, 33.

[11] PIERRE LAGUILLAUMIE, *Sport & repressione* (Roma: Samonà e Savelli, 1971), 62. Orig. *Sport, culture et répression*. Paris: Maspero, 1968.

[12] JOHN MILTON HOBERMAN, *Politica e sport. Il corpo nelle ideologie politiche dell'800 e del 900* (Bologna: Il Mulino, 1988), 269. Orig. *Sport and Political Ideology*, Austin: University of Texas Press, 1984.

[13] GERHARD VINNAI, *Il calcio come ideologia. Sport e alienazione nel mondo capitalista* (Rimini: Guaraldi, 2004), 103. Orig. *Fußballsport als Ideologie*, Frankfurt am Main: Europäische Verlagsanstalt, 1970.

[14] PIERRE LAGUILLAUMIE, op. cit., 25.

[15] ROSALBA ALTOPIEDI, *"Fatti" di sport. Il doping e la doppia morale delle organizzazioni sportive* (Milano: FrancoAngeli, 2009), 38.

[16] MARC PERELMAN, *Sport barbaro. Critica di un flagello mondiale* (Milano: Medusa, 2012), 10. Orig. *Le sport Barbare. Critique d'un fléau mondial*. Paris: Michalon Éditions, 2008.

[17] R. Barthes in JOHN MILTON HOBERMAN, op. cit., 169.

[18] BENEDICT ANDERSON, RICHARD O'GORMAN, *Imagined Communities: Reflections on the Origin and Spread of Nationalism* (London / New York: Verso, 1983).

Sports and nationalism

1. Made-up communities of millions of people, as noted by Hobsbawm, appear more real when distilled in just a few "players". Yet, although they declare themselves rooted in the most ancient times, the nations developed fairly recently, as well as their associated phenomena: nationalism, the symbols and the various national histories.[1]

2. The nation-states were formed mainly in the late nineteenth century, along with the birth of the modern Olympic Games.[2] It was Coubertin himself, founder of the International Olympic Committee, who claimed that the modern athlete exalts his own country, his own race and his own flag,[3] as well as to choose the colors of the Olympic logo among those present in all the national flags of the time. The modern Olympic Oath, written by Coubertin and introduced in 1920, cited: «We swear that we will take part in the Olympic Games in a spirit of chivalry, for the honor of our country and for the glory of sport».

3. The flag and the national anthem, the most important symbols, are also very young, since they all date back to the late eighteenth century. Then there are others; uniforms, military bands and parades, which are used to flaunt the power of the State.[4]

4. Showing off the symbols of belonging constitutes a form of territorial defense.[5]

5. The concept of "nation", with its borders, the territorial marking and protection of land (very common in the animal kingdom) clashes with the reality of the geological phenomena that affect all territories, such as the so-called "plate tectonics". Not only the current nations but also entire continents were not as we know them today nor will they be like this in the future. There were, millions of years ago, supercontinents like the one called Pangea, which included all the lands above sea level that are today partially separated. This is still evident in a geomorphological level in the complementarity of the continental coasts, and in which the correspondence between South America and Africa, for example, is particularly clear. In millions of years (if men will not have destroyed the Earth ahead of time) Africa will take Europe's place, Australia and Antarctica will adhere to South Africa, China will be attached to North America and the latter welded to Africa.

6. Adjacent groups are usually in fierce opposition. In sports it is a constant, which is institutionalized and exalted under the concept of a "derby". All boundaries, however, are mere conventions[6] mostly based on natural elements; seas, rivers, forests, mountains, but also economic and political factors. Today's states, which are generally regarded as something stable, are instead also changing and have seen their borders change several times within a few decades to merge, split up, break up into very small entities or, in several cases, disappear altogether. The new states, or would-be, need an international recognition that goes also, and above all, through the participation in sports events. Among the most recent cases there is that of Kosovo; self-proclaimed independent from Serbia in 2008, since 2014 it has a "national" soccer team through which it obtained in 2016 the affiliation to the European and international football associations even before a full international recognition.

7. Taking a step back in time but staying in the Balkan land, it is a common opinion that it was precisely a single and very short sports fact to have determined the breakup of Yugoslavia.[7] It was the evening of June 30, 1990 and in Firenze the quarterfinals of the World Cup between Argentina and Yugoslavia were taking place. A substantial equality led to the next round via penalty kicks, and the very last of these, missed by the Balkan captain is thought to have - with the sport elimination - shattered the smallest and dangerous residue of Yugoslavian nationalism.

8. With the formation of new States sports have always rushed to the aid of the national spirit, becoming the main catalyst.

9. Nationalism needs indoctrination, also through mystified sports.

10. Sports are an extraordinary national cohesion agent. They trigger a process of belonging to a territory through a tribal kinship, a common ideal to the whole nation, and arouse identification by means of an opposition to other nations according to "friend-enemy" mechanisms, evoking myths and legends on a common past and then channeling the emotions of the masses in aggressive key.[8]

11. Every nation observes with particular attention the sport that feels "its own" and through which it finds particular satisfaction in the victory. Likewise, it ignores the defeats in those sports considered minor, but which will probably in turn give satisfaction to other

nations where they are given greater importance. That is how sports, although they cannot satisfy most of the competitors, instead distribute doses of pride to the various nations, in a sort of collective illusion where everyone believes they are better than others.

12. The idea of a nation creaks with the passage of time. National representatives are now markedly multiethnic because of past colonialism, for natural migration flows or because the athletes perform a change of nationality seeking space in another representative. Many of those at high-levels, like any other worker, seek elsewhere for an economic realization (sometimes even sportive) and are, de facto, "recruited" by other states. It so happens that in different disciplines, table-tennis, for example, the cases of "naturalization", the acquisition of citizenship by a foreigner for the concession of public authorities, are rampant. Even the coaches, the other technical figures and the "national" leaders are often foreigners. There are frequent cases that are even paradoxical, like brothers who find themselves opposed to represent different nations in international competitions or like the recent match between Albania and Switzerland in the European Football Championships, in which the Swiss Representative was composed almost exclusively of foreigners, and about half of them were Albanian.

It is likely that in the future we will reconsider the concept of nations in the same way that today we look at the forced separation of the Berlin Wall until 1989 or at anachronistic figures like the Emperor of Japan, who until 1946 was considered of divine nature.

13. The nations need to invent, nourish and continually renew their traditions.[9] This is because they confer legitimacy, seem to have the same meaning of immutable natural laws and complying with these laws is being passed off as expression of objectivity.[10] Yet, most of the time, even traditions that appear to be old are often quite recent in origin and sometimes are completely made up.[11] Hobsbawm himself defines "invented traditions", the combination of practices governed by commonly accepted standards, and equipped with a ritual or symbolic nature, which seek to instill certain repetitive behavioral values and norms in which automatically imply the continuity with an old past appropriately selected or to a large extent fictitious.[12] Clearly these

manipulation tools are disguised under the cloak of antiquity[13] and «narcotic longing of an idealized past».[14]

14. Even the Roman emperor Augustus resorted to the exaltation of tradition for propaganda purposes. He did pretend, in fact, that the measures he took were necessary for a return to the "old Roman virtues".[15]

15. Hobsbawm places the intense flourishing of modern traditions created on purpose to establish and periodically reinforce loyalty obligations dating back to the thirty or forty years preceding the First World War, reaching the maximum intensity of the "invention of tradition" in Western countries in the period between the late nineteenth and early twentieth century.[16] New public holidays, official ceremonies of various kinds, heroes, symbols and especially sports, each element contributes to the ideological theory-building.

16. The traditions, or at least most of those that were not made on purpose, have been cancelled, since they were not considered functional or organic to the dominant ideology. Similarly, many alternative forms of physical activity and with a local type such as traditional games have fallen into disuse, repressed, turned into sports[17] or downgraded to folklore phenomena.[18] The medieval games or traditional ones typical of the lower classes like soccer, initially had few rules to be agreed upon from time to time, or had none at all. Certainly, there was no concept similar to "fair play".

17. The Olympic Games, considered the pinnacle event of the sports world, behind a façade of internationalism are actually the "festival of nationalisms", in which most nations celebrate themselves in some futile and temporary victory.

NOTES

[1] ERIC J. HOBSBAWM, *Nations and Nationalism Since 1780: Programme, Myth, Reality* (Cambridge: Cambridge University Press, 1990).

[2] ALAN TOMLINSON, GARRY WHANNEL, *Five-ring Circus: Money, Power and Politics at the Olympic Games* (London: Pluto Press, 1984), 86.

[3] MARC PERELMAN, *Sport barbaro. Critica di un flagello mondiale* (Milano: Medusa, 2012), 12. Orig. *Le sport Barbare. Critique d'un fléau mondial.* Paris: Michalon Éditions, 2008.

[4] ERIC J. HOBSBAWM, op. cit.

[5] NICOLA PORRO, *Sociologia del calcio* (Roma: Carocci, 2008), 79.

[6] DAVID STEPHEN MITCHELL, *Cloud Atlas* (London: Sceptre, 2004), 479.

[7] GIGI RIVA, *L'ultimo rigore di Faruk. Una storia di calcio e di guerra* (Palermo: Sellerio, 2016).

[8] JEAN-MARIE BROHM, *Sociologie politique du sport* (Nancy: Presses Universitaires de Nancy, 1992), 249. Orig. Paris: Éditions Universitaires, 1976.

[9] ERIC J.HOBSBAWM, TERENCE O. RANGER, *The Invention of Tradition* (Cambridge / New York: Cambridge University Press, 1983).

[10] GERHARD VINNAI, *Il calcio come ideologia. Sport e alienazione nel mondo capitalista* (Rimini: Guaraldi, 2004), 8. Orig. *Fußballsport als Ideologie.* Frankfurt am Main: Europäische Verlagsanstalt, 1970.

[11] ERIC J. HOBSBAWM, op. cit., 3.

[12] ERIC J. HOBSBAWM, *Ivi.*

[13] ERIC J. HOBSBAWM, op. cit., 8, 295.

[14] ROBERT REDEKER, *Lo sport contro l'uomo* (Enna: Città Aperta, 2003), 89. Orig. *Le sport contre les peuples.* Paris: Berg International, 2002.

[15] KARL-WILHELM WEEBER, *Panem et circenses. La politica dei divertimenti di massa nell'antica Roma* (Milano: Garzanti, 1989), 111. Orig. Düsseldorf / Wien: Econ Verlag, 1983.

[16] ERIC J. HOBSBAWM, *passim.*

[17] ALAN TOMLINSON, GARRY WHANNEL, op. cit., 83.

[18] STEFANO PIVATO, *La bicicletta e il sol dell'avvenire. Sport e tempo libero nel socialismo della belle époque* (Firenze: Ponte alle grazie, 1992), 11.

Sports and olympism

1. Neither the word nor the concept of "Olympism" existed in ancient Greece,[1] it is a caricature of the modern name of the town of Olympia (Ολυμπία).

2. "Olympic Games" is the incorrect transposition of *"Olympiakoi Agōnes"* (Ολυμπιακοί Αγώνες), which actually can be translated more faithfully with "Olympic competitions". Just think that the root of the word *"agōn"* is the same as the word "agony", something quite different from the merry and innocent word "games".
   The Olympic contests were not the only event of its kind in antiquity, but certainly the first to have a non-local reach. There is evidence that proves they date back to 776 BCE, although probably they started even centuries before. Officially, they lasted for much more than a millennium and ended for various reasons. In particular, they were prohibited by the Roman emperors Theodosius *(Flavius Theodosius Augustus)* I and II, respectively, in 393 and 426 CE. Despite having resisted even a long time after the ban, the town of Olympia was hit by multiple natural disasters (earthquakes and tsunamis) as a result of which it was covered by about eight meters of dirt.

3. Even the simple "olympic" attribution is misleading, because no modern edition was ever held in Olympia. If they were not just a parody of the old ones, you could perhaps talk about "isolympic" competitions, as all those that were held in different locations but that wanted bear the name of Olympia were called, which had become famous in all territories that overlooked the Mediterranean basin.

4. The name "Olympics", often used to indicate an edition of the competition, is incorrect. The Olympics is, more precisely, a four-year period between two editions of the (summer) "Olympic competitions".

5. Modern sports are the sons of this phenomenon, the "Olympism", which is the most successful example of the invention of tradition.[2]

6. Pierre de Frédy, Baron of Coubertin, universally known as the father of sports for being the founder of the modern Olympic Games, in reality was not. More simply he founded an association

called "International Olympic Committee" and called himself during the years the only restorer of the Olympic Games.

The idea of reviving the ancient Olympic contests was, at the time, raised often and by many, especially in England, France and Greece. So, there were really many before him that undertook the project and realized it.

The real first Olympic Games of the modern era were upheld in Athína in 1859, three and half years before the birth of Coubertin, which occurred in 1863.

Progressing chronologically, already between 1601 and 1612 a lawyer named Robert Dover, organized in Chipping Campden, England, the "Cotswold Olimpick Games" which included various types of races, jumping, throwing, fights and ancient rural practices. The name reveals an inspiration to classical mythology, toward which even back then the interest was growing. These games had annual editions until 1642, resumed from 1660 to 1852 and again from 1966 onwards.

In 1792, the political and French revolutionary Charles-Gilbert Romme proposed the restoration of the Olympic Games, and in 1796, a hundred years before the edition of Coubertin, the *"Olympiade de la République"* was held in Paris with an enormous success, replicated in the following two years.

In 1832, at the seminar "Le Rondeau" at Grenoble in France it was decided to devote the extra day in February in leap years - quadrennial even these - to the organization of sports events called "Olympic Games".

In 1833, the poet Panagiotis Soutsos suggested in a letter addressed to the Greek government to re-launch the contests that are the emblem of the independence and tradition of the newborn State.

In 1850, British physician and P.E. advocate, William Penny Brookes, organized every year in Much Wenlock in England sports games called "Meetings of the Olympian Class".

In 1852, the archaeologist Ernst Curtius declared himself convinced that the Olympic events would be reborn.

In 1856, the magnate of Greek origin Evangelis Zappas accepted the request of Soutsos, and personally financed the project, so the first Olympic Games of the modern era were held in Greece, as said, in 1859.

In the same year Brookes, influenced by what was happening in Greece, changed the name of its games to "Wenlock Olympian Games" which had their first edition in 1860. The two events, one in Greece and one in England got in touch, so much that Brookes sent money for the establishment of the most important award.

In 1863, after everything that had already happened, Pierre de Frédy baron de Coubertin was born.

Zappas died in 1865, leaving his inheritance to Greece with a mandate to organize the subsequent editions of the games with those funds.

In 1866, Ernst Georg Ravenstein, John Hulley and William Penny Brookes established in England the "National Olympian Association" for the promotion of an annual series of sporting events inspired by those of Much Wenlock. Not everyone in that basically classist society was in favor of games that, at the behest of Brookes, had to be open to all. These editions had only initial success, in London and Birmingham, but then dimmed until they terminated in 1883.

In 1870, the modern Olympic Games were held in a stadium for the first time, the Panathenaic of Athína, restored with the finances of Zappas.

In 1875, the third and final edition of the Olympic Games was held in the Greek capital.

In 1888, four years before the baron, another Frenchman, Jean-François Paschal Grousset, proposed the revival of the Olympic Games, which would give values of secularism, and social and scientific progress, as well as combating religious obscurantism. It was a conception quite different from that of the conservative Courbertin, who - in fact - took his distances.

For a long time he remained indifferent and contrary to the philhellenic spirit that permeated Europe at the time, but was instead attracted to athletic and educational aspects. Taking a cue from the French defeat in the Franco-Prussian War, he came to the conclusion that the losers did not have a proper physical condition and made a commitment to do some research to set up a system capable of improving it.

These studies did not bring him closer to Greece, but made him openly Anglophile. In particular, he was fascinated by the use of sports for educational purposes during that same century, attributed to the dean of the Rugby School, Thomas Arnold. He visited England several times, was aware of what was going on in Much Wenlock, and then he contacted Brookes to get closer to the event.

In 1890, Brookes invited Coubertin as guest of honor at the fortieth edition of his games. In the same year, after visiting Brookes, he wrote that «There was no need to invoke the memories of Greece and seek encouragement in the past»[3] although in other writings he partially recognized the merits of the English doctor.

In 1894, Coubertin organized a conference at the Paris University of Sorbonne, where he founded the International Olympic Committee by giving it the mission to revive the ancient Olympic Games.

In 1895, William Penny Brookes died.

In 1896, the first Olympic Games in the Coubertin version were held in Athína, in the Panathenaic Stadium.

Over time, he gradually downplayed and deliberately omitted what had been done by others for the restoration.

It is difficult to explain why the Coubertin version is the most long-lived of the modern era. Probably for a sum of factors; after so much preparation and help from others, the time was "ripe". In other words, a sufficiently broad interest had been created. Coubertin then proved to be a lobbyist and truly skilled communicator and was thus able to well develop his invention of tradition with a huge array of ideas, symbols, rituals and athletic practices with an ancient taste but which in reality had never existed.

The sensational archaeological discoveries in Olympia in the nineteenth century turned Greece into a trendy topic, fascinating and yet unknown. He therefore realized that he could attribute his own ideals to that mythical Greece, in turn inherited mainly from Victorian England, and see them legitimized thanks to that historical connotation and ancient tradition. However, as Pleket notes, recalling the ancient Olympic Games has produced particularly a bad history.[4]

Actually, the knowledge and the binding of Coubertin with Greece, as well as his devotion, were superficial and theatrical.[5] He went there only when necessary for the organization of the games of 1896,[6] repeatedly refused the legitimate demand of the Greeks to organize the event always in that country and on the contrary even tried in 1918 to move them permanently to Switzerland. He did not succeed, but the "Olympic Charter" of the International Olympic Committee still defines the Swiss city of Lausanne as the "Olympic capital",[7] which is a bizarre and incomprehensible concept.

The first editions of the Coubertin games were definitely farcical and approximate. In particular the second (Paris, 1900) and the third (Saint Louis, 1904) were subdued, not only because were embedded within two international trade exhibitions, but also due to the fact that the only "significant" events were deplorable racist spectacles.

In 1900, some runners got lost along the way and others in 1904 covered part of the route by car. Things did not go better in London in 1908, where runners were able to commit reciprocal misconducts during the run or in the premiere Athína, where a British tennis player took part in the competitions only because he could not find another place to play.[8] The grotesque tone of these editions was well explained in an article by Italian newspaper in which the messenger said: «Italy was represented at the Paris international competition by horses Oreste, Melopo and Montebello....».[9]

In 1906, between the III and the IV Olympics, the intermediate edition to celebrate the tenth anniversary of the restoration of the games in the Greek capital was held in Athína. Unlike the two previous editions, this was a great success and, although Coubertin refused to recognize it officially, historians agree that it was probably instrumental in saving the games from a new and even more rapid extinction.

7. All the rhetoric on the vaunted Greek amateurism does not reflect at all what happened in ancient times, but rather the desire of the aristocracy of the time to keep away the lower classes in the sporting practice. In fact it was claimed that, to remain faithful to the ideals of purity handed down by ancient Greece, sports should only be practiced by amateurs and not professionals. They were considered, however, "professionals", not only those who received money from sports like in today's conception, but whoever was forced to perform any kind of work for a living. "Amateurs" were,

hence, those who did not have to work, meaning the upper classes.[10]

8. There has never been an Olympic motto in Olympia. *"Citius, altius, fortius"* meaning "faster, higher, harder" was born with the first games of the modern era, and was coined in 1891 by Henri Didon, a Dominican priest and Coubertin's spiritual advisor.

9. The "Olympic message" *«L'important dans ces olympiades, c'est moins d'y gagner que d'y prendre part»* (the important thing in these Olympiads is not so much to win, but to participate) is the result of a number of misinterpretations and citations, misunderstandings and distortions.

    Even the Roman poet Ovid *(Publius Ovidius Naso)* in his Metamorphoses 8 CE made his character, defeated by Hercules, say: *«Nec tam turpe fuit vinci quam contendisse decorum est»* (It is not shameful to be beaten as it is much more worthy to have fought). So Coubertin in 1894, in a speech to the Society of Athína Parnassus said, «It would not be dishonorable to be defeated, but refusing to fight would» encourage the Greeks, scared that their athletes could lose.

    During the Games of London in 1908, the American Archbishop Ethelbert Talbot officiated a mass for the Olympic athletes in St. Paul's Cathedral. He was troubled by clashes between the British and the Americans and by the cult for victory at all costs that was being revealed. Therefore, in his homily he quoted the first letter to the Corinthians in a completely distorted interpretation that "the games themselves are more important than running and the prize and, although only one can boast the laurel, everyone participates with the same joy in the competition". So once again, it is all based on historical falsehoods; Coubertin actually had a markedly personality very far from the amicable and conciliatory spirit that emerges from the phrase "The important thing is not winning, but participating" by which he is commonly described.

10. The IOC logo, composed of the famous five rings (which in an earlier version were twisted to a single horizontal row, and only afterwards staggered) was created by Coubertin himself and made public in 1914. During the Nazi Games of 1936 it was passed off as an ancient symbol found on archaeological findings in Olympia and Delphoi. None of the numerous artifacts relating to these two sites actually have something similar. However, those thin circles

well represent the emptiness of good intentions that remain on the level of propaganda, while the actions unfortunately go in the opposite direction.

11. The whole ceremonial was built in modern times. The Olympic flame or torch, undoubtedly one of the symbolic inventions of the modern games, never existed. It was an idea of Karl Diem (Nazi leader) introduced in the 1936 Berlin games and never removed. It is a clumsy way to take inspiration from the sacred flame present in ancient Greek temples and *lampadedromia* (λαμπαδηδρομία), which was not part of a ceremony, but an actual race (and anyway, it was one of the few that were not even held in Olympia).

12. Although in ancient times, unlike what happens in modern competitions, musical competitions were also contemplated, there never was an Olympic anthem. This was invented only with the first games organized by Coubertin to Athína in 1896.

13. The Olympic film is another legacy of the Berlin Nazi edition games of 1936.

14. The prizes for the Olympians (meaning the winners in Olympic competitions) were in ancient times just simple olive wreaths, that came with a series of other benefits that varied from case to case and especially over time, but which included high-value consumer goods and various advantages, to the point where the athlete could live at the represented community's expenses.

    In the multitude of material awards that were planned for the Olympians, as well as the winners in the other Panhellenic contests, medals were never part of the awards in ancient times. These were also introduced in 1896, although the winner received the silver one and the second winner the bronze.

    The gold ones were made of pure metal only in 1908 and 1912. Actually, they contain only a little more than one part in a hundred of gold. They are mainly silver and copper and are worth, in the editions of the most generous Olympics, about a third of a clerical worker's monthly salary (in other less generous editions, about the salary of a working day), so rather little. Silver ones are mostly of this material (the rest is copper) and in any case are worth little more than half of the previous, therefore very little. As for the bronze, they are made of bronze, meaning copper and small amounts of secondary metals, with a total value of less than a sandwich from the major sponsor.

15. The universal participation of athletes (over ten thousand coming from over two hundred countries in the last editions) is only apparent. Forty percent of them come from just ten countries, the most industrialized powers.[11]

16. The Olympic Charter dates back only to 1978 by a regulation coming not from the time of ancient Greece but from a much more recent one in 1908.

17. The program of Olympic sports follows arbitrary rules which change over time, so much so that the only ever absent disciplines can literally be counted on the fingers of one hand.

    From 1912 to 1948, similar to the ancient contests that were held in Olympia and especially Delphoi, there were artistic competitions in the Olympic Games (for example in architecture, literature, music, painting and sculpture). In the Olympic Games in Stockholm in 1912 Coubertin himself participated and won in the competition of "sports literature" under the pseudonym of "Georges Hohrod and Martin Eschbach" and an artwork entitled *"Ode au Sport"*.

    Many sports have left the Olympic program, some of these have become folk practices such as tug of war, others simply fell into disuse like the ballgame, and others because their scope was too "local" like the Basque *pelota*, but there are also some which are very popular, such as rugby.

18. Noteworthy are also the discrepancies: gymnastics, for example, does not in fact exist outside of the games, while soccer games are a farce; from 1952 to 1980 only amateurs could participate. In 1984 and 1988, professionals could also participate (provided they had never played a match in the World Cup). In 1992, all players were able to participate, regardless of the status of amateur or professional, as long as they were younger than twenty-three years old. From 1996 onwards, the same rule applies but with the possibility to let three older players play.

19. Combating in general has very ancient origins, but the "Greek-Roman", one of the Olympic Games, despite the name, dates only to the nineteenth century.

20. Even what appears to be the Greek sport par excellence, the "marathon", never existed in ancient times, even in Marathonas, which is actually a city in Greece.

The reference here is to the legend of the Greek messenger Pheidippides during the war between the Greeks and Persians when, after traveling considerable distances running on impervious Greek territory and especially after the last and most important journey, from the plain of Marathonas to Athína to announce the victory in 490 BCE, he was able to announce *"Nenikékamen"* (we won) and, being exhausted, died.

The philologist Michel Jules Alfred Bréal therefore wrote in 1894 to Coubertin suggesting that he arrange a race with the same point of departure and destination, as it would have had an interesting ancient taste. And he added that, knowing the time it took the Greek warrior, it would have been possible to set a record. Emblematic is especially the aim of evoking an "ancient flavor" and the desire to find the record even before there was even a sport. Coubertin never denied Bréal's paternity in this case, but before the huge success of the idea he did not emphasized it much. As if not enough, there is a further distortion in the invented tradition. The distance of 42,195 km that everyone knows and that fans of this discipline laboriously run is not the mythical distance between the Greek locations. Simply it goes back to the modern edition of London in 1908, when the course was changed to honor the British royals at Windsor Castle.

21. For three centuries the ancient Olympic competitions were held in a single day, which reached five days in their moment of maximum development. In the first fifty years only one race was held, the *stadion* (στάδιον), a similar race to the existing 200-meter dash.

    Team sports did not exist in ancient times, just like the Winter Olympic competitions, which in the modern era were introduced only in 1924.

22. Paradoxically, the similarities between the ancient and the modern Olympic contests are numerous, but they are very different from those heralded by the propaganda as the legacy of the ancient pagan rites in use in ancient Greece; doping (which was available at the time), professionalism, misogyny, classism, misconduct among athletes, corruption at all levels, the complacent and bribed "journalism" (the *epinikia*), the overemphasis of those festivals, interference and political exploitation, boycotts, violence, racism, wars, master data falsification and so on, existed and were normal even in ancient Greece. Such events were often chosen as public

protests locations; the Greek philosopher *Peregrinus Proteus*, for example, committed suicide by theatrically throwing himself into the fire during the Olympic competitions of 165 CE.

«What in the meantime has become doctrine in science has not in fact yet been able to reach the general public, because ideology and ignorance of many opinion leaders form an almost insurmountable barrier. For these people, the ancient Olympia is to be saved in its apparent model function - at any cost, even at the cost of arbitrary exposure of the story».[12]

23. The "Olympism" remains to most a confused and incomprehensible notion that, paradoxically and ironically, is perplexing, especially to the most benevolent scholars towards its inventor. They feel sorry that he did not give to the idea a «theoretically outlined philosophical support»[13] or that «he never expressed on the subject in a systematic way».[14] Critics however, welcome the descriptions of Olympism proposed by Coubertin; a sort of «attitude of mind» or statements that it «is not a system, but a state of mind» and «Olympism is par excellence the glorification of youth. It is to glorify young people who gathered every four years in the ancient Olympia»[15] (which is absolutely false), having clear that the belief has always been a totally empty word, at which the Baron attributed different values and meanings over time depending on the convenience.

Olympism itself is then passed off as being a "movement" aimed essentially at promoting a philosophy of life able to place sports at the service of the harmonious development of humanity and peace. In reality it is an imperialistic ideology which has always proven to operate in a particularly optimal manner in authoritarian environments,[16] against human dignity and with null and often negative effects on the peace process among people.

24. The guardian and promoter of the Olympic values is the International Olympic Committee, a private supranational institution, headquartered in Switzerland and subject to the laws of that country. However, the rules laid down by this private organization are binding for all international sports and national institutions; Olympic committees, sports federations and all that has to do with the sport, both public and private. Therefore, a non-inclusive and non-democratic association (we will see why) is, in fact, the world government of sports.

The committee is historically composed of members who usually have little or nothing to do with sports. On the contrary, it has always been the presence of numerous aristocratic vintage men of all ranks; kings, princes, dukes, marquises, counts, and of course barons. Then there are the senior military, probably masons, politicians and lobbyists. There are even some athletes (strictly organic to the system), while women have only been present since 1981 and are always very limited, to reflect the misogyny of the founder. It is a self-proclaimed organization, closed as the members are co-opted (presented and appointed by the other members), and because it is not required to be accountable for its actions (exercise of power without responsibility).[17] Even the meetings are private and segregated. But it does not come as a surprise, given the number of prosecutions and convictions related to the members and how well-documented it is by international newspapers and books dedicated to it.[18]

The International Olympic Committee has changed much over time, from a mere circle of rich snobs - as it was in its infancy - to a real corporation of advertising, communication and marketing in the entertainment (sports) sector.

Already around the edition of the 1920 Olympics the events changed connotation and assumed a wider dimension. Coubertin himself was concerned by the constant growth of the phenomenon and feared above all that the Olympic Committee was no longer able to properly follow its "educational" original mission.[19] He refused commercialization and spectacle as the ultimate goal and would probably not appreciate the transformation into a centralized organization turned in on itself and its business, which mocks its ideals.

After a life spent in hotels and absorbed by its mission, Coubertin died in 1937 in relative solitude and hardship. In fact, he was not motivated by avarice and greed of wealth, but the celebrity status, which he reached and which continues to exert over his own merits.

What would happen next to his creature is the phenomenon known as "Olympic Gigantism", meaning the dreaded uncontrolled growth of the event size especially in terms of impact on the area, costs and consequences.

Since the appearance of the mass media, the Olympic Committee has been able to exploit its potential, reaching thanks to the "sport" expedient an unparalleled turnover.

Olympic events serve only to corporations and governments not spectators, nor the athletes.

Neither the nomination of a city to host the games, nor the assignment of the same call out involve the people who, on the contrary, are the subject and victim of tactics to produce consensus.

As has been well documented over the past decades, the gaming allocation process has been subject to acclaimed corruption cases, based on bribes and elegant prostitutes offered to members visiting the candidate cities.

When a city, through legal and illegal methods, is proclaimed as the venue of the Olympic events, it is intrinsically delivered to speculators. Those who rejoice are not the citizens but the businessmen and politicians, the only ones to derive real benefit.

All great events have a sneaky ploy to build huge construction sites designed to handle large amounts of public money. This is facilitated by the use of bureaucratic shortcuts imposed by the urgency of the trumpeted "popularity" of the events. They are therefore a "Trojan horse" to implement projects and expenses otherwise unacceptable for any community, both economically and environmentally.

Manifestations such as the Olympic Games are actually intended and promoted by very tight political-economic-financial lobbies, emphasized by the media for convenience or more often by simple ignorance and kindly accepted by public opinion. This, uninformed about the huge social and economic costs, has no reason to oppose what looks like a beautiful world party but which is actually a way to make huge interests otherwise unacceptable.

Even a single newly-built Olympic stadium has really exorbitant costs; equivalent to the sum of the average monthly salary of several hundreds of thousands of people. But how many, among the resident population, play sports there following the event? This applies to all facilities built for such "special occasions" even when they have not fallen into neglect, how many can be used by the citizens? An infinitesimal percentage. At best, they are used for sporting events and other types of shows.

Some of these events are known to have put States on their knees. Aware of the risks based on the experience of others before them, the citizens of Los Angeles in 1984 opposed the public funding of the Olympic Games, which on this occasion were supported by private funds. Something similar also happened during the allocation race of the 2024 Olympic Games, from which Toronto, Boston and Hamburg were withdrawn at the behest of shrewd administrators or citizens undergoing consultation. It is obvious that when you index a referendum providing all the necessary information, the response of the people is firmly against. But often, they do not have the chance to express themselves and they get to suffer the consequences.

Expenses for Athína 2004 multiplied compared to forecasts, and those for London 2012 have grown to the point of having to resort to other public funds dedicated to services who should have instead contributed to the welfare of citizens.

Olympic events, especially winter ones, reveal opportunities to deface the environment without the need for special permissions and above all without ever consulting the opinion of citizens that should accommodate and "enjoy" these festivals and the related infrastructure in the following days. On the contrary, this power is exercised by force and any voice of dissent is silenced. The apparent "importance" of the event is used as a crowbar to break up any obligation, rule or control which for any other circumstance would be strictly applied.

The Olympic Games are essentially financial transactions made with other people's money (the population) to ensure larger returns to a very limited number of beneficiaries.

As funds for most part of the construction of facilities, lots of public funds arrive, then are managed by the few who are organizing the event, meaning those people belonging to the interests of the most powerful economic groups.

A large part of the bodies involved in the top-level sports event is formally *nonprofit*, yet they have a turnover of large corporations.

During the preparation phase and the ideological redesign of the city, a wild mechanism is enacted in which we must build as much as possible as quickly as possible. Sites are open day and night with workers housed onsite so that they can always be available to work. Subcontracting and labor exploitation to increase the profit margin resulting in violation of human rights are the norm, just as workers paid with a daily wage equivalent to a kilo of bread.

Human rights are trampled not only by the slavery practices carried out towards those who have the misfortune of having to work for the Olympic machine, but prior to the initiation of the events a human cleansing takes place of all those people in need - often children - who are normally in any city, but during the games they must disappear because seeing them would upset the tenor of the party, damaging the meticulously created image of fiction. To do this, fences have been used several times with the aim to cover up entire neighborhoods and urban areas, whose extreme poverty is considered equally uncomfortable and damaging to the environment of universal well-being that must be conveyed.

Behind the reasons for a growing need for security, cities are literally militarized, which makes residents feel like it's a state of war.

In addition to the debts and to rising housing costs, the urban legacy of these events are aseptic cities, more and more equal to others as if they were made with a mold. They have the same styles, the same stores and restaurants, because they are the work of the same hand and the same cold capitalist ideology.

Once the two weeks of collective madness elapse, the "circus" is closed and the funds finished; what remains are raped environments, desolate buildings, distorted and unrecognizable places, oversized facilities impossible to manage and use, as well as a debt that turns into more taxes imposed on the population for the decades to come.

At this point, the enormous destructive machine moves like a hurricane to another city to be twisted and cemented.

To expand the sale of the product, "new markets" will then be obsessively sought, resorting to every means possible. Countries are legitimated with obvious problems on the respect of human rights like in the case of Beijing 2008, referring to which, the president of the international committee enthusiastically stated that thanks to the games it would be open to the world's largest market, China in fact.

On that occasion, the insignificance of human dignity before the economic power materialized. Instead of imposing a real change to the country in respect for human rights, the whole world not only adapted, but took advantage of the favorable environment resulting from the exploitation of human labor.

In the development plan, thanks to the absolute power of the Chinese leaders, the destruction of the old part of the city was carried out, wiping out vulnerable segments of the population just because residents in central areas, canceling their places and their stories.

In many cases it was done without even informing the residents, or through beatings to accelerate the evictions by the construction companies. The most "lucky ones" received a paltry and non-negotiable sum in exchange.

The Olympic Games leave behind evidence of facilities never used, because of excessive overhead, or simply because they are useless. The countries that have hosted such events have found themselves paying off debts for decades, also recording a drop in economic growth, employment and tourism.

Precisely the tourism sector is widely cited as one of the main recipients of the benefits. In reality, as stated by the parties concerned, not only during the mega events does it not occur a sensible visitor increase, but in many cases they complained about a decline due to the lack of traditional tourists, frightened by the wave of people and by the elevation of all costs.[20]

The prospects of job occupation - that the scarcity created by capitalism has turned into a valuable asset - are emphasized as an additional great benefit of the events. In reality it is, of course, an employment with a very limited duration. Alongside these temporary workers then there is a real army of volunteers, who with their unpaid work guarantee a further slice of exploitation to the organization, albeit consensual in this case.

In the face of so much destruction, each country gets a "sweetener", that is to say the possibility of celebrating a more or less large number of futile medals to have prevailed in as many sporting competitions, without considering having inevitably lost in the majority of the other.

Behind the hypocrisy of a fake apoliticism and promotion of pacifism, it appears embarrassing the collusion and connivance that the International Olympic Committee has had, throughout its history, with dictatorships of every kind.

Coubertin wrote in a letter that he did not appreciate Mussolini, but intensely admired Hitler as «the wheel of a new Europe and perhaps a new world».[21]

During the Olympic Games of 1904, the so-called "anthropological days" were organized, meaning competitions in which people of what used to be considered an inferior ethnic background were forced to compete against each other: Pygmies, Amerindians, Inuit, Mongols, with the aim of ridiculing them.[22]

Still in 1942, the law of the Italian Olympic Committee cited: «Tasks of the Italian National Olympic Committee (CONI) is the organization and enhancement of the national sports and to address it to the athletic training, particularly with regard to the physical and moral improvement of the race».[23]

The Romanian despot Ceauşescu and the Bulgarian Živkov were even awarded the Olympic Order. Uday, the son of the tyrant Saddam Hussein and known for his inclination to torture, was the president of the Iraqi Olympic Committee. Similarly Muhammad and al-Sa'adi, sons of the dictator al-Qadhdhafi, were respectively presidents of the Olympic Committee and of the Libyan Football Federation.

25. Many similarities with the Olympic Committee are found in its major sports federations, the International Association of Athletics Federations (IAAF) and the *Fédération Internationale de Football Association* (FIFA), whose mega event, the World Cup, follows the same bleak script.

    The international athletics federation turned out to be - from its peak - an active part in the pipelines of criminal corruption and doping on a large scale. As the international football federation, in spite of its own motto, "For the Game. For the World", it certainly does not work for the good of the world, or for the game of soccer, more or less reduced to the rank of American wrestling, a show that everyone knows to be planned and staged, but still has quite an extensive fan base.

    On the agenda is fraud, from those to get management positions, (exercised then by anachronistic tyrants), to those to address the outcome of the meetings. In addition there are cases of nepotism and bribes for assignment of events to the host countries, whose criteria seem to be very flexible according to the needs of the highest bidder. One case above all is the issue of the 2022 World

Cup in Qatar, on whose victory the newspaper The Sunday Times published[24] evidence of corruption in the form of correspondence and bank documents.

The huge turnover and money around the most widespread sporting spectacle in the world naturally puts the latter in contact with the types of crime both homogeneous (sports betting) and heterogeneous (drug cartels). But leaders of the international football federation have been able to reach the lowest levels by earning even on the misfortunes of others. In the occasion of the arrest of some of those who had stolen the funds intended for Haiti - affected in 2010 by an earthquake that caused hundreds of thousands of victims - the attorney general declared: «The betrayal of trust that is set forth here is truly outrageous, and the scale of corruption alleged herein is unconscionable».

26. The leaders of the Olympic committees and federations should have no outside work assignments in the same field, but actually many of them "collaborate" with private companies sponsoring the same sporting events, creating a full conflict of interest.

27. The Olympism strategy consists of the everlasting search for new markets possibly predisposed to the proven practices of exploitation of poverty, corruption, repression, overbuilding and militarization.

28. As opposed to the ideology of the Olympic Committee, there were also antagonists games, organized by the international workers movement. These were held between 1921 and 1937 (Prague, Frankfurt, Vienna, Chicago and Barcelona then moved to Antwerpen), also experiencing good success.

29. The important thing is not to participate but to get the most profit.

30. Olympism is the capital to such a degree of accumulation that it becomes mystified sport.

31. According to the founder of the Olympic Committee, «sport is the religion of the excess».[25] This idea is dumb and deeply dangerous, because it is the only idea of sports that has been given to the world.

NOTES

[1] DAVID C. YOUNG, *The Modern Olympics. A Struggle for Revival* (Baltimore / London: Johns Hopkins University Press, 1996), 67.

[2] ERIC J.HOBSBAWM, TERENCE O. RANGER, *The Invention of Tradition* (Cambridge / New York: Cambridge University Press, 1983).

[3] DAVID C. YOUNG, *Further thoughts on some issues of early olympic history* (Journal of Olympic History, Fall 1998).

[4] MOSES ISRAEL FINLEY, HENRI WILLY PLEKET, *I Giochi olimpici: I primi mille anni* (Roma: Editori Riuniti, 1980), 125. Orig. *The Olympic Games: The First Thousand Years*. London: Chatto and Windus, 1976.

[5] John Lucas in DAVID C. YOUNG, op. cit., 72.

[6] DAVID C. YOUNG, op. cit., 59.

[7] INTERNATIONAL OLYMPIC COMMITTEE, *Olympic Charter* (Lausanne, 2011), 31.

[8] ALAN TOMLINSON, GARRY WHANNEL, *Five-ring Circus: Money, Power and Politics at the Olympic Games* (London: Pluto Press, 1984), 20.

[9] Vanni Loriga in GIUSEPPE BRUNAMONTINI, *Esercito e Sport. Dal gesto individuale del guerriero mitologico all'educazione sportiva dei giovani di oggi* (Bari: Laterza, 1989), 183.

[10] For more details on the topic, please refer to chapter "Sports and work".

[11] MAURO VALERI, *Stare ai giochi. Olimpiadi tra discriminazioni e inclusioni* (Roma: Odradek Edizioni, 2012), 6.

[12] KARL-WILHELM WEEBER, *Olimpia e i suoi sponsor. Sport, denaro e politica nell'antichità* (Milano: Garzanti, 1992), 11. Orig. *Die unheiligen Spiele. Das antike Olympia zwischen Legende und Wirklichkeit*. Zürich / München: Artemis Verlag, 1991.

[13] ROSELLA FRASCA (a cura di), *Religio Athletae. Pierre de Coubertin e la formazione dell'uomo per la società complessa* (Roma: Società Stampa Sportiva, 2007), 30.

[14] *Ivi*.

[15] ROSELLA FRASCA, *Il corpo e la sua arte. Momenti e paradigmi di storia delle attività motorie, da Omero a P. de Coubertin* (Milano: Unicopli, 2006), 210.

[16] Michael R. Real in JIM PARRY, VASSIL GIRGINOV, *The Olympics. A Critical Reader* (New York / London: Routledge, 2008), 232.

[17] ANDREW JENNINGS, *The New Lord of the Rings. Olympic Corruption and How to Buy Gold Medals* (London: Transparency Books, 2012), 61.

[18] ANDREW JENNINGS, *Look Who's Coming to London. Meet the Real International Olympic Committee* (London: Transparency Books, 2012).

[19] Deanna Binder in JIM PARRY, VASSIL GIRGINOV, op. cit., 391.

[20] EUROPEAN TOUR OPERATORS ASSOCIATION, *Olympic Report* (London, 2012).

[21] LOUIS CALLEBAT, *The Modern Olympic Games and their Model in Antiquity* (International Journal of the Classical Tradition, Vol. 4 n.4, Spring 1998), 555-566.

[22] BROWNELL, SUSAN (edited by), *The 1904 Anthropology Days and Olympic Games: Sport, Race, and American Imperialism* (Lincoln / London: University of Nebraska Press, 2008).

[23] Legge 16 febbraio 1942 n. 426 *"Costituzione e ordinamento del Comitato olimpico nazionale italiano (C.O.N.I.)"*. Gazzetta Ufficiale n. 112 del 11.05.1942.

[24] Published on 01.06.2014.

[25] PIERRE DE FREDY DE COUBERTIN, *Pédagogie sportive* (Paris: Crés, 1922).

Sports and religion

1. Correspondence between sports and religion is nearly total. For many people, sports are what religion should be and it certainly can be considered a new form of religion, therefore the «new opium of the people».[1] Its effects and the collective emotions on the followers of the two phenomena are similar. The supporter of modern sports, Coubertin himself, defined its spirit and underlying value system *"religio athletae"*.[2] «For me sports were a religion with church, dogma, cult [...] but above all religious sentiment. [...] Today I have reached and exceeded the age at which you can freely proclaim your own heresies, I am not afraid to confess my point of view».

2. Sports perpetuate the representation of the typical dualism of some religions; in particular Zoroastrianism - the oldest among existing ones - and Christianity, influenced by it, and which later became the dominant cult.
    In the competition among athletes or groups, these are then identified by the faithful-spectators, through mechanisms usually subjective, like "good" and "evil" in their eternal struggle.

3. Today's use of cups in the award ceremony comes from ancient Greece. The Homeric poems and numerous vase paintings show that metal supports, with three legs for cauldrons or other containers, were primarily offered as a gift to the gods and victorious athletes.

4. The terminology that describes the characteristics of the two phenomena is the same;[3] it is about sacrifice, punishment, idolatry, dedication, faith, miracles and rituals.

5. The pre-Colombian communities of Mesoamerica practiced *Ōllamaliztli*, an old "ballgame" with religious and political (sometimes replacement of the war) significance. Two groups of athletes faced each other in front of the priest in a fronton and, as can be seen in the carvings found, at the end some of the participants themselves were sacrificed to the gods - according to predetermined rules - by decapitation.

6. Ortega y Gasset saw in the predatory attitude of the earliest forms of societies composed of hordes of young people used to the abduction of unrelated women, features and similarities that led him to theorize "The Sportive Origin of the State".[4] Certain,

however, is the *religious origin of the sport*. The athletic competitions of antiquity that inspired the current sports, in fact, constituted the culmination of the religious celebrations inside which were placed and the sacrifice (this time not capital) contemplated in them is the same that is found as a fundamental value of modern sports.

7. Both have a schedule of well-planned celebrations.

8. The cyclical nature of the sports season is similar to that of the natural seasons that also gave rise to superstitions which later became structured religions. For a long time, the common calendar that marked the lives of people looked back at the Olympics, starting with the first one determined in 776 BCE.

9. Pope John Paul II, one of the most incisive of the popes declaimed political history: «In Corinth, where Paul had brought the message of the Gospel, there was a very important stadium, in which the "Isthmian Games" were disputed. Therefore, appropriately, the Apostle, to spur the Christians of that city to work hard in the "race" of life, refers to athletics competitions»[5] and in the same homily, he added: «Every Christian is called to become a strong athlete of Christ». In fact, Paul of Tarsus (*Paûlos / Paulus*, said St. Paul) in the "First Letter to the Corinthians" used the sports metaphor to convey his message: «Do you not know that in a race all the runners compete, but only one receives the prize? Hence run so that you may obtain it».[6]

10. Religion and sports have heroes and legends to celebrate, and in any case each "follower" is convinced that his own party is the "right" one.

11. Both cults have devoted buildings and sites such as churches, mosques, synagogues and sports facilities, all in some way deemed "sacred" and in which to celebrate their respective functions.[7] It may happen that in the course of time one can take the place of the other. St. Peter's Basilica in the Vatican, for example, was built in the mid-seventeenth century CE above the circus wanted by the Roman emperor Caligula *(Gaius Caesar)* and completed by Nero *(Nero Claudius Caesar)* around the mid first century CE. The obelisk that stood in the center of the circus is the same that you can still admire in the center of St. Peter's Square in front of the same Basilica in the Vatican.

12. Not infrequently, the sports shrines are named after - for direct or indirect reasons - religious figures like the saints. The stadium of

Napoli for example, is called "San Paolo" to celebrate the supposed first landing of the Christian missionary in Italy.

13. Both cults have a vast array of souvenirs and objects that symbolize devotion, designed to keep the sacred alive after a pilgrimage.[8]

14. Even in modern sports it is common to encounter direct or indirect references to religion; the cross, for example, is present in numerous badges. Then there are clubs that are avowedly a confession. Emblematic is the case of Glasgow in Scotland, where the two most titled football teams in the country have a different religious orientation; Rangers (Protestants) and Celtic (Catholics).

15. Both are managed by structured and rigidly hierarchical organizations.

16. Both are capable of involving large masses of people and some sports, such as soccer, have a number of loyal fans similar to those of one of the most followed religions in the world, and even a much more heterogeneous diffusion of each other cult.

17. Although they are themselves a religion, sports does not conflict with traditional ones and indeed is to them - especially Roman Catholicism - complementary and functional. Coubertin came from a fervently Catholic family that, by educating him with the Jesuits, directed him towards an ecclesiastical career. Sports such as basketball and volleyball were born in Christian organizations (in both cases the YMCA, Young Men's Christian Association) whose members spread around the world the new game by bringing their religious message. Rimet, founder of the Soccer World Cup (that for a long time bore his name), claimed that sports, and especially soccer, were the best way to spread "Christian virtues",[9] around the world, a mission carried out later also in Brazil (and beyond) by the so-called *"Atletas de Cristo"*. Actually, precisely the Soccer World Cup, noted Comte, is a universal assembly with the entire humanity centered around the chalice (the Rimet cup in fact) that the winners, just as the priests during the harvest do, raise towards the sky.[10] But from this ceremony - disputes Redeker - «does not derive any spiritual or cultural message, no hope for humanity, no promise of improvement of one's own condition. It only celebrates the cult of advertising brands and the law of the strongest».[11]

18. Supporters and contestants, and believers and religious officials, practice rituals of various kinds to feel they have control over what happens to them, to believe they can seek refuge from adversity and ward off misfortune.

19. Athletes often resort to prayers, acts of devotion, talismans, amulets and other superstitions before a match. The coexistence of multiple forms of superstition such as the use of both superstitious rites and of its precepts of any confession seems to be considered acceptable and somewhat normal. For Bertrand, the champion himself «is nothing but the image of the glorified Christ in his redemptive martyrdom»[12] in what could be considered - and it was done for a long time in human history - a punishment of the body as an object of temptation and sins.

20. Modern sports embraces the worst aspects of religion: prejudice, irrationality and fanaticism.

21. Fanaticism detectable in the two areas is the highest. However, it is easier to expect a religious change rather than sportive.

22. Inside sports - as well as religion - practitioners/followers differ in belonging to disciplines/sects, each of which is characterized by its priests and rituals.

23. The vagueness of Olympism, which is the basis of modern sport, reflects the vagueness of religions.[13] It is always about having to blindly believe in things that conflict with reason and for which huge amounts of money are used.

24. Both are basically useless and counterproductive for the people.[14]

25. Superstition, an essential element in both cases, is the best way to govern the masses.[15]

26. Sport and religion contribute, although in different ways, to maintain the status quo. The first guarantees a constant distraction of the masses; the second induces passive acceptance of social injustice that characterizes life on earth by promising deferred bonus in an illusory "afterlife".
    Both are useful only to the dominant ideology, which is that of the ruling class. To resize the sports religion as the illusory happiness of the people is to demand their real happiness.

NOTES

[1] JEAN-MARIE BROHM, *Sociologie politique du sport* (Nancy: Presses Universitaires de Nancy, 1992), 18. Orig. Paris: Éditions Universitaires, 1976.

[2] PIERRE DE FRÉDY, DE COUBERTIN, *Mémoires olympiques* (Lausanne: Bureau International de Pédagogie Sportive, 1931), 102.

[3] DANIEL L.WANN, MERRILL J. MELNICK, GORDON W.RUSSELL, DALE G. PEASE, *Sport fans: The psychology and social impact of spectators* (New York / London: Routledge, 2001), 198.

[4] JOSÉ ORTEGA Y GASSET, "El origen deportivo del Estado" (1924), *Obras Completas*, Vol. II (Madrid: Ed. Taurus, 1963).

[5] IOANNES PAULUS PP. II, *Giubileo degli sportivi*, 29 ottobre 2000.

[6] 1 Cor. 9:24.

[7] The interchangeability between the church and the stadium as a place of worship is well represented by the possibility of celebrating, in the latter, functions like marriage, which historically belong to the first.

[8] Slowikowski & Loy, 1993 in Alan G. Ingham in RICHARD GIULIANOTTI (edited by), *Sport and Modern Social Theorists* (Basingstoke: Palgrave Macmillan, 2004), 27.

[9] JOE HUMPHREYS, *Foul Play: What's wrong with Sport* (London: Icon Books, 2008), 48.

[10] Auguste Comte in ROBERT REDEKER, *Lo sport contro l'uomo* (Enna: Città Aperta, 2003). Orig. *Le sport contre les peuples*. Paris: Berg International, 2002, 13.

[11] *Ivi*.

[12] Ginette Bertrand in PIERRE LAGUILLAUMIE, *Sport & repressione* (Roma: Samonà e Savelli, 1971), 89. Orig. *Sport, culture et répression*. Paris: Maspero, 1968.

[13] Lamartine DaCosta in JIM PARRY, VASSIL GIRGINOV, *The Olympics. A Critical Reader* (New York / London: Routledge, 2008), 70.

[14] http://headtale.com

[15] Baruch de Spinoza in JEAN-MARIE BROHM, *La Tyrannie sportive. Théorie critique d'un opium du peuple* (Paris: Beauchesne, 2006), 227.

Sports and work

1. Sports find real reason to exist in the playful, unproductive character and well-being that comes from practice. Nevertheless, what is sold as such presents none of these aspects. From an activity carried out for fun or recreation, the modern sports are and represent the exact opposite.

2. At the origins of modern sports of Olympic mold, a class banning practice reigned, which was only allowed to "amateurs", considering only those people who did not carry out any work because they did not need it for a living. It was a sneaky ploy to exclude the lower classes from competitions, moreover based on a completely false assumption; the one for which athletes in ancient Greece were aristocrats who were dedicated to competitions exclusively for *kalokagathia* (καλοκαγαθία) and *areté* (ἀρετή), therefore an ideal of both outer and inner perfection and excellence. This was a noble spirit which later degenerated between the fifth and fourth centuries CE due to the advent of "professionalism". This thesis was carried out by the Olympic Committee and supported publicly by Brundage, one of his best-known (and discussed) presidents.

It is known instead that there was never an "advent" of professionalism, because this matter was consistent in ancient sports.

Admirably, Young,[1] in disassembling piece by piece the Greek myth of amateurism in athletics, also outlines three confused and contradictory versions about the definition of "amateur" that have been proposed over time:

An amateur is an athlete who does not draw financial gain from sports; anyone who does is a professional. An amateur devotes little time to sports and has a short career; a professional is constantly training and has a long career. An amateur is a born "gentleman" or otherwise belongs to the highest socio-economic class; a professional is an athlete of the working class. Yet, the word *"athlētés"* (ἀθλητής) itself always meant literally, «one who competes for a prize», while the ancient Greeks had no idea what the concept of "amateur" was and therefore they did not even have a word to describe it.

It was an interpretation by Victorian ideals, performed by the classicist scholars of the time (Gardiner, above all), to allow that ancient Greece be used «to give a lesson to the modern man».[2]

In reality, both noblemen and not took part, and everybody accepted awards.

3. Every practice that can be included among the pleasant things, like sport, stops being a pleasure and becomes a duty when it is held by constriction and without spontaneity which, in turn, will make leisure time paradoxically necessary. Instead of being an alternative to work, modern sports come as the "continuation of the work" (Adorno). Professional athletes in a particular sport, in fact, will engage in an entirely different sport during their free time.

   Huizinga noted in his "Homo Ludens" that «the player's attitude to the profession is no longer a real playful one, the spontaneity and the idea of hobby do not apply to him anymore. Gradually sports in modern society move away from the pure sphere of the game and become an element *sui generis*, not play, but not seriousness» and that «despite being very important for participants and spectators, it remains a sterile feature where the most traditional fun factor has died».[3] Afterwards, Caillois[4] defined the games in general (and most sports are) as assets free of obligations, carried out in times dedicated to them, with an uncertain outcome, subject to specific agreements between participants, fictitious compared to the normal life and especially unproductive in terms of material and economic return.

   We are thus faced with a modern sport that goes from being a game to becoming the «obligated reproduction of the game»,[5] which sounds inhumane as it would for example having to fulfill a sexual act by constriction.

4. The deeper the level of involvement in the organization of sports, the greater the proximity to the scope of employment. The concept is clear to the athletes themselves, who are the first who use the word "work" when speaking of their activities.

5. Even remaining within the "free time", it is extremely difficult for people to practice sports for pleasure, out of preconceived ideological schemes that provide regimentation, with all the resulting constraints.

6. In a capitalist system, sports fall in the entertainment industry and represent the largest component.

7. Like any other worker, the athlete serves to create surplus value and profit for the owners of the workforce, which show and sell advertising respectively to spectators and advertisers. A high-level athlete's training time is equivalent and is sometimes greater than the working time (commonly measured in hours/man). In both cases, shorter and shorter times of execution are required that flank the productive worker to the successful athlete. Both exchange their labor power for a wage and the other party expects a financial return on investment.

8. Athletes who mostly live the sport-work constriction see the victory as the simple fulfillment of a duty. Commonly, workers in a broad sense seem satisfied with their condition because they have interiorized the repression.

9. A career in sports is very short and intense for obvious biological limits. Rarely does this allow the athlete to even get an alternative cultural and work preparation. This forces the sports worker to accumulate as much money as possible - often illegally concealed from the tax authorities - to cope, when out of the "scene", for a very uncertain future. Those who fail require a reintegration plan in the work field, just like what happens with former long-time prisoners.

10. Behind the hypocrisy of the (false) amateurism wanted by the upper classes, a pro in disguise exists today. The sports system maintains a façade of apparent purity by pretending that everything that is carried out is not work. But in sports nothing is as it seems, so, if the high-level athletes do not appear as workers, who really works in the sports field must be content with receiving compensation often reduced in the form of reimbursement of expenses, allowances and must find a second job, this time "official".

11. Even in companies operating outside of the sports field, the inherent prerogatives of competitiveness, teamwork, subordination and order execution, are welcome and encouraged.

12. The rigidly organized sports environment has similarities with the business world, as to appear like perfect duplication. There are colleagues/teammates, each with a role and a salary based on both individual and team performance. There is a pyramid organization with a Taylorist division of tasks. Not coincidentally, Taylor himself, to expose his theory, used parallels with sport. The

Principles of Scientific Management, based on the rationalization of the production cycle, were implemented through the decomposition and fragmentation of production processes in the individual constituent movements made by the workers to achieve maximum performance. Standard lead times were assigned to these movements.

The mechanization of the sports work involves motor learning by the athlete of the most effective and efficient movements in order to produce the best performance achievable with the biological capacity given in terms of millimeters, fractions of a second or other forms of performance. This occurs first through the obsessive repetition of the single and simpler parts which are broken down, to then be accomplished entirely and correctly in sequence. This applies also in team sports, where, in addition to individual quality, it is necessary to study the test patterns of the "game". Such stereotypical sequences of fractional operations represent the way in which athletes are, in fact, "programmed" to the production of the show with a sport motif that is perceived by the public as "sports".

13. The worker and the sportsman, dehumanized and mechanized become «appendages of a production process that does not belong to them»[6] and mere executors of that set of means learned to perform a motor action in the most effective way (technical[7]).

   The conception of human being as a tool to fulfill functions (lift, throw, push and so on) with the highest possible performance demands - although with a few exceptions - is a strict selection, classification and prioritization based on morphological characteristics.

14. Typical transpositions of the business world to the sports are the division of tasks - well represented by the team sports - and specialization, as a result of which the athlete, if he wants to live up to it, must specialize not in a discipline but in a single "specialty" which requires scientific and consistent training.

   Managers and leaders at various levels deal with the organizational part and simple workers/athletes to whom is requested manpower. This repetitiveness further contributes to the process of transforming a man into a machine.

   Just like in sports fields, also in the factories, in particular in those where work on the assembly line is present, the flooring is delimited by colored lines indicating the work area/game and scoreboards identical to those of the athletics competitions are present. Instead of athletic performance, the performance is shown in terms of production; usually times and quantity.

For both athlete and employee figures there are specific footwear and clothing, sometimes produced by the same companies who sponsor elite athletes with astronomical figures in order to sell to the masses of humble workers.

15. The concept of work is presented in sports and through sports always in a positive light.

   In a predatory system based on scarcity, the profuse effort of the athlete-hero evokes and celebrates the one expressed in business, considered, in whatever form (alienating, inhuman and dehumanizing, frustrating, underpaid, downgrading) a precious and indisputable asset, maximum aspiration and *raison d'être* of men.

16. In Bucciarelli's analysis on sports as a phenomenon of alienation or of liberation, the relationships within it are characterized by two aspects; the contractual one, to which men are bound together more by convention than for communion, and the competitive one, in which everyone is a competitor of the other.[8] The same relations are found in the working sphere, where individuals are together for contractual obligations without a liking or a mutual choice, and simultaneously put into competition with each other.

NOTES

[1] DAVID C. YOUNG, *The Olympic Myth of Greek Amateur Athletics* (Chicago: Ares Publishers, 1984), 182.

[2] *Ibidem*, 76.

[3] JOHAN HUIZINGA, *Homo ludens* (Torino: Einaudi, 1949), 231. Orig. *Homo ludens. Proeve eener bepaling van het spel-element der cultuur.* Haarlem: H.D. Tjeenk Willink, 1938.

[4] ROGER CAILLOIS, *Les jeux et les hommes. Le masque et le vertige* (Paris: Gallimard, 1958).

[5] *Ibidem*, 10.

[6] PIERRE LAGUILLAUMIE, *Sport & repressione* (Roma: Samonà e Savelli, 1971), 51. Orig. *Sport, culture et répression.* Paris: Maspero, 1968.

[7] GEORGES VIGARELLO, *Culture e tecniche dello sport. Gesti, strumenti, materiali, organizzazioni: un'antropologia dei fenomeni sportivi nella società contemporanea* (Milano: il Saggiatore, 1993), 16. Orig. *Une histoire culturelle du sport.* Paris: Éditions Robert Laffont, 1988.

[8] CLAUDIO BUCCIARELLI, *Lo sport come ideologia: alienazione o liberazione?* (Roma: AVE, 1974), 104.

Sports and entertainment

1. What is served up as the only form of sport it is actually the total denial. This is clearly a "spectator sport" run by a real entertainment industry. The more the events develop in a capitalist context, sold as top-level sports and take a wide reach, the more they move away from being sports and are placed in all respects in the context of the performance.

2. The mega-events such as the Olympic Games and the World Cup are the largest *non-sports* but sedentary events of the world. Because for every athlete who competes, there are millions of sedentary people watching it, in an enduring transfer athlete (active sportsman) - spectator (passive sportsman). Precisely those "millions of sportsmen sitting down" mentioned by Provvisionato, which, in lieu of a sports for everyone that sees them as protagonists of their own activities, they receive a passive "sport",[1] capable of giving only compensatory satisfactions for the non-lived lives, allowing even the "losers", the victims of a markedly predatory society, the fleeting feeling of having won.[2]

3. The sporting show and the sports practiced are inversely proportional. The most affected populations to the first are less likely to approach regular physical activity, and they end up suffering the consequences.

4. "Sports" are not only a form of entertainment, but it is the show par excellence and its success is multifactorial. First it enjoys a propaganda like no equals; all are subject to environmental conditioning hard to escape from for a harmonious integration into society. The omnipresence; the calendars of each discipline are dense of official meetings that take place all year round. In rare exceptions "friendly matches" are held aimed at maintaining the training, testing technical solutions and above all to raise money while on tour for a fee just like those of the stars of a musical show. The media coverage is so remarkable that the number of other workers in the wake of the events can exceed that of the athletes involved. It so happens that broadcasters, thanks to the presence of multiple television channels - some of which are dedicated exclusively to sporting shows - arrive to broadcast more hours of sports than there are in real life. Albeit ephemeral, the sporting show has the advantage of lending itself to a common celebration:

easily comprehensible, simplified further by countless comments and self-styled experts reconstructions; the diversity of real life; the ability to arouse many different emotions. The strong point compared to most of the other shows is the uncertainty of the ending, while being aware that there is never actually an end. An athlete or a team, whether they win or lose, never undergoes the final victory or defeat, as a result of a continuous series of endless twists and turns.

5. From the Olympic Games of Rome in 1960, the modern sport, from a "live" show, officially became a television genre. For the first time the broadcast covered twenty countries, while today it reaches well over two hundred.

   Through this abominable union between two elements that should be antithetical, television and sport, puts in place a massive global campaign of physical and sporting miseducation.

6. The epochal events that mark the world almost disappears behind the frequency and intensity of communication related to sporting events.

7. Symbolically, the producer of the Olympic ceremonies on the occasion of the Barcelona Games in 1992 called it «the longest advertising message of his career».[3]

   As for any other advertising, what matters most is the number of spectators. That because of this is inflated by including the "potential" ones, which are simply located in an area having access to television or that have casually seen only a part of the event. Everything is put into the pot to have important figures like those over a billion usually declared on the occasion of the World Cup or the Olympic Games.

8. The live audience and those who make use of the show through the media fulfill two very different functions:

   The former, although they represent now only a negligible part of the proceeds, are important for the free contribution and actually paid for the creation of a solemn atmosphere. For this reason, they are vital, sometimes as much as the athletes on the field for a successful event and symbolically, on the occasion of the most important ones, the public and athletes photograph each other. The absence of a public therefore is particularly a problem of image and when it happens, you run for cover in a laughable way; installing in half-empty stadiums silhouettes of spectators that give from a camera shot the semblance of normality and not show the low importance of the match and by broadcasting from the speakers the noise of a nonexistent crowd. A great part of the public that still physically participates, in addition to a show, looks for a place where in turn they can "show off", like much of the organized cheering, that is done both peacefully and not, but also the occasional one, that has a carnival spirit.

The second are fundamental since they guarantee the achievement of a high return. The crucial role of the latter was revealed in 2005 when, during the World Ski Championships in Bormio in Italy, a giant slalom race was canceled because of the impossibility to broadcast via live television due to a strike of the shooting technicians.

9. When attending a sports event in person you immediately realize that you are, in fact, inside the scene of a TV drama show staged on a (sportive) reality.

10. In the mega-main event of the capitalist country par excellence, the United States, you can find the essence of the capitalist sports' concept. The so-called Super Bowl, the final event that awards the title of champion of the professional league football, is a meeting in which the seal of the athletes betrays a violent character, diluted in a sea of advertising, exaltation, shows such as music and dancing, all topped off with the obligatory nationalism. The nature, anything but sportive, of the event is witnessed by the fact that this is the second day where people consume more food in the United States, after Thanksgiving Day.

11. Significantly, in many countries the "professional sport" is, in the social security level and pertaining to labor law, combined with the work in the show.

12. As with any other type of television, even the sporting show is subjected to the analysis index of the audience, through which the companies involved can learn and capture the audience's interest. The same information, combined with the ability of a discipline to attract advertising, determines the admission or expulsion from the sport that counts. Among the most famous victims of such spendable television (as well as its very anachronistic nature) is the struggle, among the most ancient disciplines of human history and of primary importance in the ancient contests where the Olympic machine claims to take inspiration from.

13. There is an unofficial hierarchy of sports practices; some have a diffusion and a sequel at an international level that leads them to be considered more important than those restricted to a mere local significance level. So far nothing odd, but the hierarchy of which we speak does not follow that logic at all, but rather that of the attractiveness of the show produced. Soccer is a simple example as a sport of primary importance, but it is so particularly for its entertainment qualities, because even in countries where it is most loved, it has an equal, and sometimes even lower, number of practitioners than those of the fitness, which instead (having no spectacular value) is not even officially recognized as a sport.

14. Just as there are sports in decline, new ones are born precisely from the combination of media and companies wishing to promote themselves. These may be more spectacular variants of existing disciplines or entirely new practices, but what matters is the presence of a strong spectacular value.

15. The technological evolution of the media has resulted in a substantial convergence between the sporting show industry and that of the video games. The former one integrates real pictures with virtual reality images, while the latter has reached such levels of realism that it is increasingly difficult to distinguish one from the other.

16. The dominance of mass communication on modern sports is demonstrated unequivocally by the regulatory changes that each discipline has undergone. The show requires certain times, so that the schedule can be met, and breaks in order to insert advertising. To meet the needs of the media the timetable which is provided for the contemporaneity of the meetings has also been sacrificed. Due to the fragmentation on more hours of the day and in more days, the sporting show has filled every void possible and viewers can constantly feed their addiction. Sports fans, who are "emotionally involved consumers", [4] represent a type of particularly valuable customers for businesses. Having loyalty as primary characteristic, they lend themselves more or less unconsciously to exploitation.[5] To put it as Turano, «a fever is a disease and some people are killed by diseases while some people are enriched by them».[6]

17. The worship of the sample-star of the sporting show corresponds to a debasement of one's being, the identification with it is a sad depersonalization of the self.

18. After a relatively short career for almost all athletes, regardless of the discipline, the aspiration of many of those who despite having reached the highest levels have failed to secure a sufficient income, it is to exploit their sporting popularity to recycle themselves in the nearby entertainment and advertising world.

19. Sports language is constantly excessive and emphasizing, to enhance the perception of the importance of what they can't have. It obsessively represents in speed sequences and the most spectacular technical moves in different angles to make them "epic". It accentuates the differences and divisions between "good" and "bad", and "us" and "them" to polarize the audience's emotions. Finally, it provides continuous performance statistics of the protagonists, perpetuating the obsessive quantification of performance.

20. The sporting show is subject to the same deteriorating dynamics of the movie house and well described by Silvano Agosti;[7] every human being is born with an aggressive, extraordinary, unique creativity that is annihilated as a function of a more comfortable approval. The power apparatus invents the "sportsman", someone having a combination of features that allows him to stand above the masses. The latter are unfortunately only deserving of infinite compassion, because as a small, miserable, humiliating assets they have the residual liberty of clapping their hands.

NOTES

[1] SANDRO PROVVISIONATO, *Lo sport in Italia. Analisi, storia, ideologia del fenomeno sportivo dal fascismo ad oggi* (Roma: Samonà e Savelli, 1978), 73.

[2] GERHARD VINNAI, *Il calcio come ideologia. Sport e alienazione nel mondo capitalista* (Rimini: Guaraldi, 2004), 18. Orig. *Fußballsport als Ideologie*, Frankfurt am Main: Europäische Verlagsanstalt, 1970.

[3] Michael R. Real in JIM PARRY, VASSIL GIRGINOV, *The Olympics. A Critical Reader* (New York / London: Routledge, 2008), 230.

[4] NICOLA PORRO, *Sociologia del calcio* (Roma: Carocci, 2008), 85.

[5] JOE HUMPHREYS, *Foul Play: What's wrong with Sport* (London: Icon Books, 2008), 165.

[6] GIANFRANCESCO TURANO, *Fuori gioco. Calcio e potere. Da Della Valle a Berlusconi, da Preziosi a Moratti. La vera storia dei presidenti di Serie A* (Milano: Chiarelettere, 2012), 7.

[7] TURRINI, DAVIDE, *Silvano Agosti: Il cinema è in agonia e gli spettatori mi fanno una pena infinita*, Il Fatto Quotidiano, 7 luglio 2016.

Sports and power

1. The sporting spectacle has always been the best ally of the established power. It makes a significant contribution to the acceptance and maintenance of the status quo in the oppressor-oppressed relationship, meaning the exercise in repressive key of the power taken away from the population by a small ruling class.

2. «History teaches, but has no pupils»,[1] wrote Gramsci. The political use of the competitive events dates back to the times of the *Polis* in ancient Greece, but it is in Imperial Rome that these become a fundamental governmental instrument with multiple functions. They allowed, in fact, the emperors to probe the popularity of its measures by the general public-people, and just like the *Saturnalia* (religious festivals precursor of the carnival) represented an outlet of the popular discontent and the resulting aggression. They also constituted a moment of contact with subjects and a way to influence them with the idea of somehow having voice in public life. To put it as Carcopino: «A nation which yawns is ripe for revolt. The Caesars have left yawning Roman plebs, neither of hunger, nor of boredom: the shows were a great diversion to the unemployment of the governed, and, consequently, the safe tool of absolutism».[2]

This practice, as carefully documented by Weeber,[3] did not escape the harsh criticism of the writers and orators of the time. The most incisive was that of Juvenal *(Decimus Iunius Iuvenalis)*, which he called *"panem et circenses"*[4] (bread and games [circus]) these concessions aimed at the renunciation of power and rights by the people, but also Pliny the Younger *(Gaius Plinius Caecilius Secundus)*, Tertullian *(Quintus Septimius Florens Tertullianus)* and especially Seneca *(Lucius Annaeus Seneca)* did not fail to note the general enthusiasm for shows that Livy *(Titus Livius)* came to define as "unbearable madness".

At that time, the whole symbolic apparatus had not yet been developed, the one capable of instilling a sense of belonging as it does in the current sporting spectacle. However, four different colors to distinguish the *factiones* (equivalent of today's teams) were introduced for the first time in circuses *(ludi circenses)*, inviting viewers to take sides with either of them. The first two, the *albata* (white, symbolizing the winter) and *russata* (red, representing the summer) were followed by *prasina* (green, of course evoked the spring) and *veneta* (blue, symbolizing autumn). These were later joined by the *purpurea* and *aurata* (purple and gold, respectively). The impulse towards cheering, towards rivalries and towards the clashes between supporters of rival *factiones* was remarkable because siding with an unchanging color was infinitely less demanding than following charioteers and horses, which inevitably changed over time.

In the relatively short life of modern sport, this has taken over all the functions already absolved in ancient times and has always acted as supporter, accomplice, instrument of propaganda and distraction of the new totalitarian regimes.

Fascism was able to grasp these great potentials by transforming the pride and belonging arising from soccer victories of the national soccer team into political consensus, as well as creating around the head the image of the sport par excellence, and therefore a kind of superman.

Nazism recognized its propaganda effectiveness and made large use of it. The Berlin 1936 Olympic Games offered a very broad spectrum of its application and Hitler himself did not miss the opportunity to personally proclaim the opening in front of the world.

In the aftermath of the massacre that took place on October 2, 1968 in Ciudad de México - where anti-government student protests were suppressed by the army who fired on demonstrators and passers - the Olympic Committee ignored the incident and still allowed the show to start.

The dictator of the Democratic Republic of Congo Mobutu was able to host the eagerly anticipated match in Kinshasa for the world title of heavyweight boxing between George Foreman and Muhammad Ali.

The South American military regimes, those of Castelo Branco, Pinochet Ugarte and Videla, for example, took full advantage of this instrument. During the 1978 World Cup in Argentina, the military junta of General Videla was able to exercise all its violence even a few meters away from the stage, and thanks to the success of the national soccer team (on which also weigh strong suspicions of corruption) was able to consolidate its dictatorship. The Brazilian self-legitimized and reinforced national unity through the construction of stadiums and the dispute of a large number of sporting events.

Back to Europe, General Franco not only proclaimed the opening of the games in Spain, but also held the opening speech of the 63rd Congress of the International Olympic Committee next to his President Brundage [5] and nationalistic political leaders of the former Yugoslav republics utilized sports to create consensus around separatist projects.

The last president of the North Korean Roh Tae-woo with military origin, inaugurated the Olympic Games in Seoul, the only ones held in that country.

The Chinese capitalist-communist regime has long undertaken massive programs targeted exclusively at obtaining the greatest number of medals. Since the demonstration of superiority through better ranking in the medal is the only goal of every competitor, some of them go to the extremes to get it. Children are taken away from their families and subjected to a life exclusively made of training in disciplines for which they do not harbor any interest and often are not even historically practiced, but which, on the basis of specific studies, are more likely to win.

Even the monarchies less prone to sporting events have had to approach it to increase their consent, as well as pseudo "Western democracies", whose rulers see in sports an important element of communion with the people.

3.   The sporting spectacle is not just the most important mass media,[6] but also a clear geopolitical phenomenon. The new countries announce themselves to the people of the world through their national football team, quickly gaining recognition and legitimacy.

4.   Attending sporting events is far from being a free activity. Buying a single ticket involves a variety of prohibitions the implementation of which, in fact, depersonalizes the possessor reducing it to what really matters, his mere functions of a useful viewer-piece of a televised choreography and of course a consumer.

5.   The repression and the violation of individual liberties also take origin from trying to defend business interests and huge investments of the sponsors. For example, the Olympic Charter expressly prohibits any form of religious or political advertising or manifestation, not only in competitions but also in surrounding

places, which in any case should be free since they are public. Added to these is the prohibition of consuming products other than those of the sponsors and any manifestation of dissent towards these events - if they can somehow put them in a bad light - are banned even inside their homes.

6.   The sports spectacle constitutes, together with the culture of work, which in turn reflects and fuels, one of the two pillars that support the dominant system.

The deception relating to employment is the one for which, despite the enormous technological advances that make any work much more effective, the duration of the actual time of average work is maintained at around a third of the day. This overemployment of the population causes job scarcity (and above all the salaries that follow) hence the need for money. That is how something usually unpleasant (even a duty) is perceived as valuable and coveted. People, once the work day is over, emptied of their mental and physical energies, must devote a short time and their remaining strengths to their daily life tasks, leaving only the desire to be able, as soon as possible, to disengage the mind and body.

This function is performed by the sporting spectacle, the most insidious and powerful of the weapons of mass distraction, manufacturing consent, control and social depoliticization, because it was considered universally positive and above any suspicion. It helps to unload the frustration and promotes apathy, resignation of the masses and the renunciation of critical thinking. Both the practitioner and the viewer are constantly indoctrinated to respect the hierarchy and submission to social institutions and the dominant classes, which thus perpetuate its hegemony. The total enslavement and the uncritical acceptance occurs when the ideological apparatus succeeds in internalizing and identifying people with the system of rules imposed on them.[7] In the words of Bourdieu, «the most effective form of power is the one that appears to those who suffer as the natural order of things» and therefore we find ourselves moving "freely", but within a logic of slavery.[8]

Sports creates an apparent "identity of interests between rulers and ruled"[9] that not only thwarts hostility and claims, but also increases the inequities and the gap between the two categories. The greater the economic and cultural distance between the classes, the more pronounced the level of involvement and euphoria of the poor towards the sports phenomenon.

Even Chomsky has repeatedly denounced in his writings, that the people are offered something unimportant to attend to and above all the illusion, just as they did in imperial Rome, of being involved in the collective importance.

Citizens therefore, openly deprived of precious time from work and deceitfully from entertainment, are effectively stripped of political sovereignty.

7. It is not uncommon for top athletes, at the same level of showmen that are not part of the sporting spectacle, to become nominees for political office at the end of their careers thanks to their popularity. In both cases, it is once again a devious trick to bring votes to their parties through what in political jargon are called "useful idiots".

8. Not surprisingly, all the hierarchical institutions, for these reasons, exalt the sport spectacle. The Church, for example, in the Pope's words, said «Sport [...] prevents deviations of the cult of the body [...] it will help, above all, to become citizens of the social order and peace lovers».[10]

NOTES

[1] ANTONIO GRAMSCI, *Italia e Spagna*, Ordine Nuovo, 11 marzo 1921, anno I, n.70.

[2] JÉRÔME ERNEST JOSEPH CARCOPINO, *La vita quotidiana a Roma all'apogeo dell'Impero* (Roma / Bari: Laterza, 1971), 239. Orig. *La vie quotidienne à Rome à l'apogée de l'Empire.* Paris: Hachette, 1939.

[3] KARL-WILHELM WEEBER, *Panem et circenses. La politica dei divertimenti di massa nell'antica Roma* (Milano: Garzanti, 1989), 7 e segg. Orig. *Panem et circenses.* Düsseldorf / Wien: Econ Verlag, 1983.

[4] There was a time when people with the plebiscite elected generals, heads of state, commanders of legions, but has now withdrawn into the shell, and only wants two things: bread and games.

[5] COMITÉ INTERNATIONAL OLYMPIQUE, *Bulletin of the International Olympic Committee*, Lausanne, 1965, 64.

[6] MARC PERELMAN, *Sport barbaro. Critica di un flagello mondiale* (Milano: Medusa, 2012), 50. Orig. *Le sport Barbare. Critique d'un fléau mondial.* Paris: Michalon Éditions, 2008.

[7] GERHARD VINNAI, *Il calcio come ideologia. Sport e alienazione nel mondo capitalista* (Rimini: Guaraldi, 2004), 124. Orig. *Fußballsport als Ideologie.* Frankfurt am Main: Europäische Verlagsanstalt, 1970.

[8] CLAUDIO BUCCIARELLI, *Lo sport come ideologia: alienazione o liberazione?* (Roma: AVE, 1974), 57.

[9] ULRIKE PROKOP, *Olimpiadi dello spreco e dell'inganno* (Rimini: Guaraldi, 1972), back cover. Orig. *Soziologie der Olympischen Spiele. Sport und Kapitalismus.* München: Carl Hanser, 1971.

[10] IOANNES PAULUS PP. II, *Udienza a Castelgandolfo*, 11 ottobre 1981.

Sports and capitalism

1. Modern sport, born in England with the industrial revolution, is exported to the world like goods and with goods, and the sportivization of nations goes hand in hand with their industrialization. The port cities are therefore the first in which sports clubs bloom and, more generally, the industrial and commercial capitals will become even those of the sport.

2. Just as capitalism is only the dominant economic system, but not necessarily the best for society, the competitive practices are consequently dominant but certainly not the best. This is because they spread a conflictual human relations model, in which the object overrides the subject and everyone thinks about themselves against all others.

3. In the configuration of the capitalist sport, people capable of realizing a show that can arouse interest in the market are hired by companies who will sell such show produced both live and especially through the mass media. In more advanced cases, sports companies come to own television stations or vice versa. Thanks to the resulting notoriety it will then be possible to sell advertising space and receive sponsorships perpetuating the combination: "extraction of capital surplus/accumulation". The discovery of this huge marketability of the sporting show brought the omnipresence and omnipotence of the capital in sports.

4. Already during the Olympic Games in Helsinki in 1952 the first marketing program linked to the event was launched and even during the 1964 Tokyo games a brand of cigarettes called "Olympia"[1] was marketed.

5. That of capitalist sports sponsorship is just an important yet subtle mechanism. The viewer-consumer, manipulated emotionally, absorbs in the context of the sporting show advertisements much more intensely than any other. The sporting show thus proves to be the ideal container in which to insert commercial advertising. The lack of intellectual effort required for this type of audience in fact allows for easier assimilation of the advertising messages, which instead would lose effectiveness if observed during programs capable of stimulating intelligence.
It also takes full advantage of the image of sports as a synonym of positivity, health, carefreeness, energy, fun and youth. To take

advantage of this are therefore mainly companies that need to reveal products as presentable which are actually not; unhealthy foods and drinks (alcoholic or not) that should have nothing to do with practiced sports (but that have much in common with the one seen on TV), banks and finance companies, insurance companies, car manufacturers, oil and gas companies, or otherwise enterprises seeking benevolence in the territory as well as companies of any kind that always aim at the positive association with sports to clean up their image.

6. The five Olympic rings are obviously a registered trademark and overprotected, the best known in the world, preceding that of the most infamous sandwiches corporation.

7. At the end of the twentieth century, the professional clubs begin to be listed. The high-level sports clubs are hence real companies with the sole purpose of having profits[2] from the sale of their sports product to the masses of consumers. Consequently, also the positions of the major sports federations and Olympic committees are predominantly occupied by executives and industry officials.

8. The buying and selling of athletes, which occurs even by subdividing them into percentage parts (in order to allow the management to be in co-ownership, thus reducing the business risk) presents itself as a modern form of a "cattle market".

9. In capitalist sports, top athletes are, in fact, single person companies[3] operating in both the sporting show and in different and often distant sectors. Some are even listed in the stock exchange, where the value of the shares fluctuates according to a set of tangible and intangible factors such as performance, income, career lengths and in general the perception of success that the professional is able to convey to the market.
    This is evident in the modern individual-level sport, less in team sports. Although in the eyes of the viewer there are groups of more or less well-rehearsed athletes, in the top-levels it is actually the individual company whose profits also depend on the goodness of the partnership (results in competitions) and the related internal hierarchy dynamics (some athletes have the status of "star" and get more than any other, who end up becoming minions).

10. Exemplifying the "success stories" of some elite athletes who, from humble beginnings have achieved success and money, capitalist sports convey a distorted and misleading message of the

"right" society, in which the opportunity to change your life for the better is available to everyone. In fact, for every case like this there is a countless number of people who have tried in vain and, even among successful athletes, those who have failed to manage well the earnings of a short career find themselves, having been squeezed, to live in complete poverty.

11. Leading American basketball companies have come to change more cities in search of greater public (customers) numbers, just like circus companies do.

12. The motor sports events, as well as the cycling "caravans", are enduring advertising campaigns designed to drive the relevant industries, causing the "standard" models buyers to dream of being like the drivers of the racing models.

13. Another reason why they "invest" in the sporting show is represented by the instant fame, the public legitimacy and the ability to communicate incisively and free to the masses through the mainstream media, all organic to the system.

14. On the occasion of the centenary of the first games in the version of Coubertin, the decision to award the event not to the logical headquarters of Athína, but to the US city of Atlanta, home of the multinational sugar drinks and historic sponsor of the event caused a stir among the faithful of the alleged Olympic idealism.

15. The omnipotence of the capitalism in sports is also well represented by the assignment of one of the two mega-events; the final phase of the World Cup to Qatar, which has no football tradition, does not have a climate compatible and above all does not recognize the fundamental human rights. But it possesses surely what matters most in modern sports.

16. The sporting press, which acts as a resonance and indoctrinates cash populations daily with this sports ideology, lives under the protective wing of industrial organizations.

17. Modern sports are a formidable device for handling huge amounts of public money and the resulting speculation through endless sites that are opened. For these crimes towards the population, even more serious ones are added; as reported by Amnesty International in fact, the construction of the facilities for the World Cup involves millions of slaves, and many of them end up dying.

18. Both the sporting practice and the passive participation in sports events receive and reproduce the class logic of the system in which

they develop. Most practices require major expenses in terms of equipment, registration and lessons. Regarding the viewers, the different sectors in which the installations are segmented reflect broadly the subdivision of society based on economic logic.

19. Even outside the sports world there is the same misconception that capitalism, intended as an economic system, perpetuates its hegemony. Not certainly due to its effectiveness, but thanks to the illusion, cultivated by most, to be able to access the wealth as some manage to do.

20. The system of sporting show needs constant and massive injections of money, but they are never enough. For this, it is kept alive "artificially" by draining public resources destined to other and more important measures (including grassroots sport) in favor of the people. For the same reason it is a sector where everything has a fee, even watching matches that are not part of the official tournaments (rightfully so-called "friendly", since in the others they are all enemies) or banal and boring workouts.

21. Capitalism has achieved, also and above all in the modern sport and through the modern sport, all that had been feared by communism.[4]

22. Like any other aspect of the consumer society, the sports phenomenon participates in the crowds and endless pursuit of growth at any cost, which imposes both the shortage and the waste, both the overproduction and the superfluous desire, finally becoming sad metaphor.

23. That which is perceived on the occasion of the mega-events, in addition to the artificial atmosphere of celebration is a police state, dictated not only by questionable reasons of safety, but also from the protection of advertising investment of the sponsors.

24. The individual counts only as a bearer of the workforce (employee) or money (consumer). Within this capitalist logic every human relationship, even in sports, is inevitably mediated and distorted by the economic exchange.

25. The rankings in competitions accurately reflect the degree of erosion of sports in the various countries by the dominant system.

NOTES

[1] INTERNATIONAL OLYMPIC COMMITTEE, *Olympic Marketing Fact File* (Lausanne, 2015), 16.

[2] GERHARD VINNAI, *Il calcio come ideologia. Sport e alienazione nel mondo capitalista* (Rimini: Guaraldi, 2004), 60. Orig. *Fußballsport als Ideologie*. Frankfurt am Main: Europäische Verlagsanstalt, 1970.

[3] Although very often they are classified as employees for tax purposes.

[4] JEFF SPARROW.

Sports and industrialism

1. If the industrial liberalism came first and then the financial one has led to the worst forms of exploitation ever existed, it is no surprise that this approach has been transferred to all that it pertains to, including the sporting show.

2. The fundamental characteristics of the various sporting practices have changed over time, even radically. This has happened for many factors, but the one certainly more incisive was the link with the industry.

3. The connection between modern industry and sports is an inseparable and constant relationship of equal exchange. The first is an important sector in which to pour the industrial product with the need to use different items and clothing for each discipline. The second, with its technological innovations,[1] allows the sporting show to maintain a high level of interest by being able to always push human limits. In the pole vault, for example, with the progress of decontextualisation by a natural environment of ditches and streams to that used in athletics, has moved gradually from wood to bamboo, aluminum and glass or carbon fiber, whose mechanical characteristics in flexibility and elasticity allowed previously unthinkable measures to be reached. The hammer throw saw the replacement of the working tool with a special and more suited tool for throwing; the technique of fencing changes profoundly with the armature removal; the starting blocks in the race made it possible to achieve maximum initial push, which was obviously unthinkable maintaining the standing position which was used from the early ancient race practices. Each new material or combination thereof and each new form affects, sometimes in a radical way, the sporting practice.[2]

4. The management of sports as entertainment industry has led to the "amputation" of its features that are incompatible with the laws of the show. The need for certain and shorter times introduced such as the so-called tie-break in tennis and volleyball, to increase the interest has determined more or less noticeable changes in all disciplines, until the adoption in soccer of balls specially realized in order to obtain unpredictable trajectories for goalkeepers, with the consequent probability of increasing the goals, salient moments of this discipline. Lowering the net in table tennis has

increased the spectacle through the extremely fast exchanges which can be realized.

5. According to the same calculations, the sports that are not considered sufficiently attractive for the public are set aside in favor of others, sometimes invented out of thin air depending on the television output and the ability to push the public for consumption.

6. In the sporting show nothing is thrown away and everything is sold. Thus, the paying public are offered, through the media, the opportunity to see what happens in the locker rooms. In addition to satisfying the morbid and peeping needs, statistics are analyzed on every measurable aspect of the match, even placing sensors inside tools, through sophisticated graphics very similar to those used in business presentations, all in the obsessive search for quantification.

7. Sports clubs, especially those listed, are clearly real businesses that pursue profits. It can even happen that sports groups born within such corporations operating in other sectors, become sports companies of the first order. This happened in soccer with the famous pharmaceutical corporation in Leverkusen in Germany and especially with the giant of electrical and electronic products in Eindhoven, Holland.

8. The bid committees to host the Olympic Games are very similar - by analyzing its members, big industrialists and politicians - to the steering committee of a big business corporation.[3]

9. The industrial capitalism manifests fully its predatory nature in the production of sporting goods, taking advantage of the needy and/or child labor, making them work in dilapidated environments for peanuts and violating human rights in many aspects.

10. You cannot better describe the influence of industrialism on sports of what was done by Notario: «Industrial civilization, which replaces the peasant one that was born from a vice of origin: in it everything is based on the economy rather than on humans. The man, in this civilization, has become the object and not the subject of the economy. [...] It is the factory of the slaves [...] intended to be all the same: uniform consumers of uniform objects. The leisure and sports therefore, in such a civilization, are not exempt from this breathless logic [...] "the need to kick back" with entertainment

provided by the industrialized culture is repressive itself. Man lives in a series of "cages" where few in the control room feature him and the "free time" runs the risk of being the last cage, the most ambiguous of all because gilded».[4] That is how the repression of the industrial model is exercised in every moment of human life.

NOTES

[1] LUIGI VOLPICELLI, *Industrialismo e sport (antisportivo)* (Roma: Armando Armando, 1960), 22.

[2] GEORGES VIGARELLO, *Culture e tecniche dello sport. Gesti, strumenti, materiali, organizzazioni: un'antropologia dei fenomeni sportivi nella società contemporanea* (Milano: il Saggiatore, 1993), 22, 126 and 152. Orig. *Une histoire culturelle du sport*. Paris: Éditions Robert Laffont, 1988.

[3] MASSIMILIANO ANGELUCCI, *Il paradosso dello sport in Italia. Le scienze motorie e lo sport per tutti* (Frankfurt am Main: Biblioteca Italiana, 2015), 204.

[4] A. Notario in CLAUDIO BUCCIARELLI, *Lo sport come ideologia: alienazione o liberazione?* (Roma: AVE, 1974), 46.

Sports and record

1. Brohm defines a record as the «supreme unit of measure» or «highest performance ever offered by a human body».[1] It is of the sought-after final stage of the "workout - competition - performance - result - measure - record" scheme which originates from the capitalist conception of modern sport. The principle of maximum efficiency is then expression within the record and from it, in turn, it is widespread and amplified as the universal concept applicable to any other sector.

2. The record represents one of the major differences of the modern conception of sports compared to the classic one which it believes it draw inspiration from, when in fact the victory was once linked only to the "here and now", without further dilated competitions in time and space, but above all without chasing the idea of an impossible infinite progress.

3. The possibility of an infinite progress, particularly when applied to the performance of human beings, represents the biggest lie and deceit of the record. This is an extreme version of an idea that is already extreme per se, one in which you have to win at all costs and in which «Winning is not everything. It is the only thing».[2]

4. Such tendency towards perfection that is perpetually out of reach and so much pursuit of victory and winners produce only countless defeats and losers, and of course «new records to break».[3]

5. Whereas human possibilities meet their limits we resort to the technological progress of the materials used in sports before reverting to seeking, in a vicious cycle, further efforts from the human body itself. At this point, in fact, in the race for perennially raised objectives and to continue to stay in the loop ensuring sensationalism, we must inevitably turn to scientific aspects, both those considered legitimate and those considered unlawful.

6. The construction of an "athlete-machine" therefore becomes a team effort by sports doctors, biochemists, kinesiologists, physiotherapists, nutritionists, massage therapists and athletes themselves, who, being the object of so much work, become in turn experts in the field.[4]

7. The winners then, in particular those who are able to establish a record, are mostly a mere combination of biological qualities

(particularly the type and amount of motor neurons and muscle fibers having somatic ideal characteristics for a given discipline) and emotional state (such as willingness to devote oneself entirely to the result obtained, even at the expense of anything else).

8. In a system which provides for the victory of a participant and the consequent defeat of all the others, the joy and satisfaction were not the most widespread mood but instead frustration and failure.

9. Even winning may not be enough if this, as far as efficiency goes in terms of results or performance, does not meet the expectations of the "experts" and the public.

10. The subtle and insidious illusion that lies behind so much resonance dedicated to the sports spectacle is that by which to the advancement of performance corresponds to a social progress.[5] Lucot notes «All the world records are announced by the written press, both spoken and audiovisual, in the same way as a new discovery to beat cancer, or a *coup d'état*. [...] In most cases, a new record causes an effect of astonishment. [...] Mankind seems to have made a decisive leap, going from the Stone Age to the Bronze Age. All for a hundredth of a second. What do these ten seconds represent in our minds, exactly? What do these 2,30m of high jump represent? Nothing, they are mere figures, abstractions».[6]
    Actually it is a trivial and repeated attempt to answer questions such as "who is the best", "who is the first", "who is the strongest", "who runs faster" or "who throws farthest" which are basically and typically childish questions.[7]

11. In his *Sociologie politique du sport*, Brohm points out how the sports story romanticizes athletes by assigning them names from the animal kingdom, thus underlining certain qualities. So the magazine Paris Match, comparing Homo Sapiens to other species in a sort of "Biosphere's Olympic Games", found the distinct inferiority in every discipline.[8] This finding did not escape even the cynical philosophers of ancient Greece: «Once Diogenes the cynic met an athlete who, with his friends and admirers, was celebrating a great victory and boasted of being the fastest runner of all Greece. Diogenes dismissed him with a joke: "But not faster than a rabbit or a deer, and they, the fastest animals, are also the most cowardly"».[9]

12. Human intelligence is not a single form of expression but rather multiple (linguistic, logical-mathematical, figurative-spatial,

kinesthetic or motor, musical, interpersonal, or social or even relational, intrapersonal, naturalistic, existential or philosophical). The motor one - basilar in sports - is an innate characteristic, and due to a large amount of cells called "pyramidal" (larger neurons able to send a very large number of efferences) and addressed to the voluntary movement, end the related synaptic connections quickly (especially with the motor neurons of the spinal cord).

Therefore, to excel in sports represents especially a superior motor intelligence, which should not be overestimated nor underestimated compared to other forms of intelligence.

13. Paraphrasing Marx, the true limit of the record is the record itself.

NOTES

[1] Jean-Marie Brohm in GIANNI BOCCARDELLI (a cura di), *I signori del gioco. Storia, massificazione, interpretazioni dello sport* (Napoli: Liguori editore, 1982), 144.

[2] Henry "Red" Sanders in THOMAS A.TUTKO, BILL BRUNS, *Winning is Everything and Other American Myths* (New York: MacMillan, 1976), 4.

[3] *Ibidem*, 2.

[4] BERO RIGAUER, *Sport and Work* (New York: Columbia University Press, 1981), 21. Orig. *Sport und Arbeit*, Frankfurt am Main: Suhrkamp, 1969.

[5] JEAN-MARIE BROHM, *La Tyrannie sportive. Théorie critique d'un opium du peuple* (Paris: Beauchesne, 2006), 119.

[6] H. Lucot in JEAN-MARIE BROHM, *Sociologie politique du sport* (Nancy: Presses Universitaires de Nancy, 1992), 322. I ed. Paris: Éditions Universitaires, 1976.

[7] H. H. HENSCHEN, R. WETTER, *Anti-olympia* (München: Carl Hanser Verlag, 1972), 15.

[8] JEAN-MARIE BROHM, *Sociologie politique du sport*, op. cit., 354.

[9] MOSES ISRAEL FINLEY, HENRI WILLY PLEKET, *I Giochi olimpici: I primi mille anni* (Roma: Editori Riuniti, 1980), 112. Orig. *The Olympic Games: The First Thousand Years*. London: Chatto and Windus, 1976.

Sports and doping

1. The use of substances or practices to improve performance is considered doping. However, the boundary between lawful and unlawful doping is unstable and constantly changing.

   The purpose of doping, although objectively futile, is to constantly shift forward the limit of human capabilities at any cost.

2. Even in ancient times, since the first festivals, they resorted to herbal teas and other natural substances then prohibited (but which today would be more than licit). The ban derived exclusively from sporting ethics, because the athlete interested in doping possessed far fewer ways to hurt himself. It is with modern sports and the use of pharmacology, molecular biology and genetics, that we must also tackle the issue related to health. The high-level athletes know that unlike the ancient sport, in which participation was open, doping is necessary even just to overcome the preliminary selections and be part of the small circle of those who can aspire to victory, without, however, being completely sufficient to obtain it.

3. Doping is not a deviance of modern sport, but it is part of it and it represents rather the deepest essence. It is a natural response, a "reflection" of the athlete to the environment (sports) around him, requiring performance beyond the normal limits through which to obtain victories or to realize ever more exciting shows, and the impossibility of being able to satisfy them with just his own body.

4. During the Olympic Games in Rome in 1960, a young Danish cyclist died during the race of sunstroke, they said. It turned out to be one of the first official doping victims. Many followed and still follow, most of them classified at best among the "suspicious" deaths. Young athletes do not have the right perception of the problem, they are not properly informed, they are blinded by the lust for victory and money, or often they are simply unaware about what they take. Numerous former world-class athletes have confessed to having taken performance-enhancing drugs without initially knowing it. A great Italian cyclist who instead took them consciously, later on minimized his actions by saying that it was basically sports medicine, which actually represents today a "licit doping".[1]

5. It is only since the late sixties that doping is considered as an unlawful practice. For prominent athletes until then it was just an innocent form of sports medicine.

6. Modern sports are fueled by flows of money, including ones from the sponsorship mechanism, which represents a major source. Companies pay to associate their name with something universally perceived as positive, in other words, sports. The farther the product is from the concepts that are associated with sports (health and well-being, joy, vitality, youth, fun, sociability, and so on) the greater the importance of this infamous bond. Not surprisingly, the major sponsors of each event are notoriously unhealthy companies that produce sugar-based drinks, sandwiches, alcoholic beverages, industrial confectionery, financial products and so on.

    However, what happens more and more often, is that the sponsors get the opposite effect to the one initially planned. The confirmed cases of doping, in fact, often end up being associated with the name of the sponsor, creating a negative association with it. In these cases, the system turns against those who have fueled it, which in turn must immediately distance themselves from this "deadly embrace".

7. The sale of drugs with doping potential is constantly growing and the phenomenon is spreading even at an amateur level, where of course checks are virtually non-existent. With a seemingly schizophrenic attitude, media and sports institutions claim respect for the rules and fair play, pretending to be interested in sports for all, but then emphasize and reward only those chasing victory at any cost. The top athlete in particular does not have much choice; submit or disappear. According to the cross-country skier Mika Kristian Myllylä who pleaded guilty, it is a situation known to all and common to all the countries governed by the rule of the top sport.[2]

8. Upon the occurrence of an important act of doping, they run for cover in two ways; if the applicable procedures allow to minimize and limit the initial damage, they opt for this solution through which everything is soon forgotten. Otherwise they resort immediately to the mechanism of the scapegoat. All those who participated in the collective exaltation of the champion do their best to discredit the individual athlete. It is important that this always happens for an athlete at a time in order not to awake the -

legitimate - suspicion that the problem is in the whole system, rather than being an individual and isolated decision of a few "bad apples".

9. It is deeply hypocritical that sports organizations will constitute themselves as the injured party against the athletes guilty of having used doping.

   After being discovered and having served some time in prison, the founder of a renowned laboratory in San Francisco specializing in doping confessed to having provided all the participating athletes in a major final of the hundred-meter dash and confirmed the propagandistic nature of the race checks instead of at least nine months before, when they actually would be needed.

   Nevertheless, the sporting environment is extremely conspiratorial. According to the claims of an Italian magistrate it is even «easier to find a repentant in Mafia trials than in doping»[3] and also as a result of precise dossiers, such as the one presented to the Italian Olympic Committee by Alessandro Donati, the problem is not being addressed. Donati himself - among the best Track and Field technicians and an expert against doping - who has published books[4] on the subject, denouncing the facts and figures, was excluded from the sports system.

10. The British newspaper Sunday Times and the German issuer ARD, having come into possession of confidential documents of the International Association of Athletics Federations about thousands of blood tests carried out in the first decade of this century, they have reported and produced the documentary "Doping - Top Secret: the Shadowy World of Athletics / Geheimsache Doping".

    The most qualified experts on anti-doping, called to examine the values reported, have deduced an extraordinary diffusion of deception by the athletes during the greatest global sporting events.

    A third of the medals (including many gold medals) won in endurance sports at the Olympic Games and world championships were obtained from athletes whose tests have given rise to suspicious results. In some final matches, even all three athletes on the podium showed blood tests of this kind. One of the scholars questioned said about this: «Never have I seen such an alarmingly abnormal set of blood values. So many athletes appear to have doped with impunity, and it is damning that the IAAF appears to have idly sat by and let this happen».

11. In the face of proclamations for the battle against doping, it is actually a phenomenon tacitly accepted by the governments of the sport, necessary so that they may feed the followers the exceptional stories that they accustomed to expect. Thus, the top athletes themselves notice the anomaly of not being subjected to anti-doping for long periods. There are events, in fact, that take place without any checks because each organizer fears of "staining" their own event with any positive results. In addition, the anti-doping costs are so high that make it possible only in big competitions and after the race, ignoring the checks during the preparation periods away from the race, those in which doping practices are more concentrated. As Altopiedi denounces, even in mega-events such as the Olympic Games, the doping percentages found range between 0.8 and 2%. According to these numbers, one could argue that doping in sports is almost non-existent. For sports organizations, however, the expected optimal situation is that doping exists (otherwise there would be no interest in modern sports as they have been designed) but it must not take too visible dimensions, such as to undermine the credibility of all its components. So, in an in-depth discussion on the subject, [5] Altopiedi disputes that the sports organizations are more oriented to the management of the public rhetoric than to the limitation of the phenomenon itself. Governments have to give the impression that something is being done without actually taking action. Between "saying" and "doing" there is and must necessarily be a certain distance. [6]

Moreover, we must remember that historically the most massive doping practices are precisely those implemented not by individual diverted athletes, but by the states. There are innumerable testimonies of experts about the "state doping" that, for most people, is an integral part of high-level competitions. Paradigmatic is the case of the German Democratic Republic, whose president, Erich Honecker, was even honored by the president of the Olympic Committee for the extraordinary results of his athletes. Athletes that we found out later to have been an army of about ten thousand people subjected to the most massive state-doping campaign to demonstrate essentially, as in the recent case of Russia, the superiority of "East" on "West".

12. In a sad parable, the cyclist Armstrong became the most successful ever, secured the admiration of the whole world (as well as substantial sponsorships) not only as the winner of the Tour de France, but by establishing the additional "record" in the conquest of seven consequent editions. It was unimaginable feat in an event of this magnitude, which for almost a month involves the whole country. Once discovered that it had been not a prodigy, but (of course) a doping case, he made public confession in an interview with the most-watched television program in the United States, using words that should open the eyes of dreamers. When asked «Was it humanly possible to win the *Tour de France* without doping, seven times?». The answer was «Not in my opinion. That generation. I did not invent the culture, but I did not try to stop the culture. [...] I did not have access to anything else that nobody else did».

When he was asked: «Was everybody doing it?», He replied «I did not know everybody [...] There will be people that say that, "Ok, there are two hundred guys on the Tour, I can tell you five guys that did not, and those are the five heroes", and they are right».

Again «To keep on winning it meant you had to keep taking banned substances to do it? Are you saying that is how common it was?». «Yes, and I am not sure that this is an acceptable answer, but that is like saying we have to have air in our tyres or we have to have water in our bottles. That was, in my view, part of the job». Finally, in the account of the moment when the sponsors began, one after another, calling the cyclist telling him they did not want to have anything to do with him, we feel all the hypocrisy of a profoundly distorted and doped sports system.

13. Who is so cynical to accept this sport, should welcome equally serenely the existence of doping, fighting for its legalization and rejoice for those records and "epic" benefits dependent thereon.

NOTES

[1] Jean-Marie Brohm in GIANNI BOCCARDELLI (a cura di), *I signori del gioco. Storia, massificazione, interpretazioni dello sport* (Napoli: Liguori editore, 1982), 23.

[2] Mika Kristian Myllylä, self-confessed drug cheat in ROBERTO BOSIO, *I giochi del potere* (Cesena: Macro Edizioni, 2006), 40.

[3] Raffaele Guariniello, prosecutor of Torino in LORENZO VENDEMIALE, *Olanda, in tv documentario sul doping nella Juve anni '90 (con troppe omissioni)*, Il Fatto Quotidiano, 28 maggio 2013.

[4] ALESSANDRO DONATI, *Campioni senza valore*. Firenze: Ponte alle Grazie, 1989.

[5] ROSALBA ALTOPIEDI, *"Fatti" di sport. Il doping e la doppia morale delle organizzazioni sportive*. Milano: FrancoAngeli, 2009.

[6] N. Brunsson in ROSALBA ALTOPIEDI, *Ibidem*, 103.

Sports and alienation

1. Far from being the expression of personal individuality, the modern sport, and in particular the top one, operates a full depersonalization of the athlete who, as a human being, should be the measure of all things while in fact he himself becomes a measuring instrument.[1]

2. Developers of Critical Theory sensed that sportsmen are - in fact - reduced to mere quantitative values[2] (milliseconds, meters, goals, baskets, aims, points, and so on) related to their performance. In some sports like baseball, statistics (in this case called "sabermetrics") surge to the main reason of interest. In each discipline, however, athletes are not considered as people, but "bodies" which, notes Brohm, after being classified into categories of sex, age and sometimes weight are accurately measured in organic functions and anthropometric characteristics, evaluated and compared with other bodies in order to select the best, that is to say the most suitable for the purpose. The human dimension is cancelled in favor of the function of the body as a mere tool.

3. Faithfully to the line of sports commercialism, athletes are transformed into "bins labels and self-propelled advertising space"[3] before being identified primarily with numbers. The names, where present, are due solely to cold needs for promotional sales.

4. The sports facilities, among the biggest "non-places"[4] of each city, are the factories[5] in which a mass of "non-persons", the audience, observes other "non-persons" used as race cars, jump points, and of course money.

5. In the "society oriented to the conquest"[6] sports, made up of cut-throat competition and struggle for existence, the sense of transience, loneliness, insecurity, uncertainty and isolation become natural reactions of the individual-athlete.

6. In the events of mystified sports, simple yet dehumanizing social relations are implemented. Multitudes of people are concentrated in a limited space, yet more isolated than ever, shouting uniform and meaningless sentences, demanding victory and showmanship from other people under the brutal condition for which the winner is worth something, and who loses is not worth anything.

7. Paraphrasing the evergreen Orwell, modern sports are a sedentary lifestyle, leisure is another slavery, ignorance is consensus, victory is defeat, and the record is oblivion.

NOTES

[1] CLAUDIO BUCCIARELLI, *Lo sport come ideologia: alienazione o liberazione?* (Roma: AVE, 1974), 70.

[2] GERHARD VINNAI, *Il calcio come ideologia. Sport e alienazione nel mondo capitalista* (Rimini: Guaraldi, 2004), 31. Orig. *Fußballsport als Ideologie*, Frankfurt am Main: Europäische Verlagsanstalt, 1970.

[3] SANDRO PROVVISIONATO, *Lo sport in Italia. Analisi, storia, ideologia del fenomeno sportivo dal fascismo ad oggi* (Roma: Samonà e Savelli, 1978), 95.

[4] ZYGMUNT BAUMAN, *Modernità liquida* (Roma / Bari: Laterza, 2002), 113. Orig. *Liquid Modernity*, Cambridge / Malden: Polity Press, 2000.

[5] Lewis Mumford in JEAN-MARIE BROHM, *Sociologie politique du sport* (Nancy: Presses Universitaires de Nancy, 1992), 154. I ed. Paris: Éditions Universitaires, 1976.

[6] David C. McClelland in BERO RIGAUER, *Sport and Work* (New York: Columbia University Press, 1981), xxxiv. Orig. *Sport und Arbeit.* Frankfurt am Main: Suhrkamp, 1969.

Sports and education

1. The fact that sports are a fundamental element in childhood is now known. For example they contribute to an improvement in cognitive functions and of course predispose a physical form which will keep away possible insidious risk factors in adulthood. For these and other reasons, every parent feels compelled to encourage their children to take an interest towards one or more sports. However, the model of sports offered to young people internationally is unfortunately far from being the bearer of any benefit.

2. It is paradoxical that the sports system proposed to the majority of young people around the world comes from the old-pedagogical ideal of Coubertin, who spoke of "manly sports" and wrote that «...hand combat and punches - especially the punches - are not devoid of a certain utility in high school. Teachers should never endorse such behavior, but if they are smart, they'll know when to ignore them in some cases».[1]
    He was in turn inspired by the work of the ecclesiastic dean of the School of Rugby Arnold,[2] who was not only an advocate of an authoritarian style and favorable to corporal punishment, but whose "pedagogy" was simply to select students by removing those "less promising" to conform the rest to the "unwritten rules" of social life, exalting the «masculinity, honor, patriotism and religiosity»,[3] but especially to institutionalize and functionalize the violence that reigned in the relations among students.

3. Kids can play spontaneously for hours without caring about who is winning, simply for the pleasure that it brings.[4] Instead, in sports organized by adults indoctrinated by the ruling system, young people find a very different reality from the one that amused them. Parents project onto children the desire for a sporting career even at the expense of a happy childhood. Improvisation becomes a distant memory, and they start to train consistently and rationally. The word "game" is drained of meaning and remains only in the name of some sports but, as revealed by Vinnai, expressions such as "football game", "player", "playground" or "game rule" have become consequently illusory.[5]

4. The young athletes, who began playing in their early years of life, are often trained through fear, treated as miniature adults and, in

fact, instigated by the coaches and the environment to mutual competition, with a high risk of developing aggression and narcissistic features, of course, as well as an alarming individualism. In such education based on performance, the question that is often asked in households is not "Did you have fun?" or "How did you play?" but "Did you win?".[6]

5. Accustomed since the beginning of their sports experience that it is organized to the concept of "employment" and the value it can assume based on performance, then subjected to the deeply distorting example of the stardom, young people are likely to easily deceive themselves and develop a kind of "anxiety for quick and substantial gains",[7] accompanied by an arrogant and whimsical personality, like that of the famous examples they are offered. Young (real or fake) promises coming from problematic countries see a structured opportunity for social redemption in sports, but they end more easily in a modern and different "slave trade". In any case, it seems of interest to no one that for every young, new champion on the sports scene they silently sacrifice a vastly superior number.

6. In an interesting monograph[8] on youth abandonment, Bortolotti establishes an incidence that in certain disciplines reaches shares close to fifty percent. The reasons are attributable in some way to the inhumanity of that "natural selection"; for example, the shame of losing against a teammate or the bitterness of defeat, as well as the inability to express the "required" aggressiveness in a competition.

7. The only real education offered by the capitalist sport, one that we truly want to give, is the one that shapes future producers and consumers.

NOTES

[1] PIERRE DE FRÉDY DE COUBERTIN, *"L'Éducation de la paix"* in La Réforme Sociale, 2 série, tome VII, 16 Septembre 1889, 361-363.

[2] Whose knowledge, in reality, was only superficial and distorted as originating almost exclusively from reading a book: Brown's School Days by Thomas Hughes.

[3] ROSELLA FRASCA, *Religio athletae. Pierre de Coubertin e la formazione dell'uomo per la società complessa* (Roma: Società Stampa Sportiva), 48.

[4] Salomon Asch in PIERRE LAGUILLAUMIE, *Sport & repressione* (Roma: Samonà e Savelli, 1971), 15. Orig. *Sport, culture et répression.* Paris: Maspero, 1968.

[5] GERHARD VINNAI, *Il calcio come ideologia. Sport e alienazione nel mondo capitalista* (Rimini: Guaraldi, 2004), 29. Orig. *Fußballsport als Ideologie*, Frankfurt am Main: Europäische Verlagsanstalt, 1970.

[6] THOMAS A.TUTKO, BILL BRUNS, *Winning is Everything and Other American Myths* (New York: MacMillan, 1976), vii.

[7] MICHEL BOUET, *Les motivations des sportifs* (Paris: Éditions Universitaires, 1969).

[8] ALESSANDRO BORTOLOTTI, *Sport addio. Perché i giovani abbandonano la pratica sportiva* (Bari: La Meridiana, 2002), 111.

Sports and detriment

1. In the popular imagination, sports are good for the health, and, in general terms, this is true. However you must consider that "sports" is an umbrella term; "sportive" is the practitioner, but "sportive" also refers to the fan who sits and watches, and "sportive" is the bet he places, as well as, those who are neither practicing nor passionate, dressing in a "sportive" style, by not wearing elegant clothes, or driving "sportive" cars despite the fact that these facilitate a sedentary lifestyle like any other. This extent of meaning opens up the way to an accidental or deliberate confusion.

   In the modern sports system itself, like in a pyramid, the sports summit exists, that "for the few", in which a precisely limited number of particularly gifted athletes and professionals usually achieve a form of entertainment, and the basic sport, the one partly practiced by the mass especially for fun and salutatory purposes. In sports declination in the capitalistic key, this is mainly entertainment, a propaganda tool, a means of control and regimentation, a gimmick for the creation of great works and unnecessary demonstrations. These are all interpretations that want top sports to prevail over the grassroots ones. Logically, public funds dedicated generically "to the sport", the money of the population, is quietly bestowed on the sports form that does not offer them any benefits.

2. If you want to enter seriously in competitive sports, you have to be willing to destroy yourself.[1] Out of the ordinary, in fact, the actual practice of organized sports has many more shadows than lights. First, the excess that this necessarily implies is never the bearer of benefits and every athlete, even if amateur, puts into account the possibility of suffering injuries, even serious ones, like the natural state of things. Depending on the different practices you encounter in general there are extremely dangerous postures, abnormal consumption of drugs (especially painkillers and performance-enhancing drugs), frequent need for medical support, unbalanced eating habits, and "legal" but despicable and sometimes deadly tricks, like the so-called "weight cut"[2] up to the "new frontiers" that could be represented by the use of implants, surgery or pain-related mechanisms, without which you can

withstand higher maximum efforts that would otherwise be unreachable, risking major damages.

3. The training, initially mere repetition of the movements to be performed, has become intensive, a bodily mortification dependent on a possible victory[3] that sometimes occurs within national projects even against the will of the athletes. In all other cases, the sporting purpose seems to mitigate if not erase the awareness of the risks connected to certain stages of training or practice that can end up developing a cult of suffering, a masochistic pleasure in dominating your own body, in taking it to the extreme. The athlete is «happy about his bad luck» argues Perelman.[4] In bodybuilding there is the slogan "no pain, no gain" (of muscle mass) but it is in general that have the concepts of "sacrifice", "effort", and "duty". In other social environments these concepts are experienced negatively or with annoyance, yet in the sports world they assume the function of values not only necessary but also positive.[5]

4. Aside from defining the Games' characteristics, Caillois[6] classified them in four different types; *agon* (competition), *alea* (luck), *mimicry* (mask) and *ilinx* (vertigo). Most of the modern sports usually present the first two, occasionally even vertigo (for example in skiing), and more rarely the mask.

   Today they try to minimize the importance of casualty (*alea*, a Latin word to literally indicate the dice) and maximize that of the commitment, of constant training, of strict discipline. While these attitudes certainly contribute to a favorable orientation of the final outcome, luck still has a great ability to influence. Suffice it to say, even before the matches, there is the phase of the drawing and pairing of contenders, the weather conditions that can favor the characteristics of one competitor over another, or even the timing of the season in relation to physical training (sometimes optimal at the end, in other cases at the beginning but with a subsequent bending) and so on with all the infinite possible variables that follow. The perennial attempt to establish hierarchies, superiority, and records cannot be really satisfied and remains something ephemeral. In such a context, basic sports that are oriented toward the actual welfare of the population, exist almost exclusively as a form of aspiration to the top sports.

5. In front of the myth of eternal youth and the "superman" that evokes modern sport, you can just see that, unfortunately, our hero-athletes are human beings with a biological path and a life expectancy not much different from those of all the others.

6. Some disciplines have a probable direct connection with serious illnesses; amyotrophic lateral sclerosis, for example, (also known as "Lou Gehrig's disease", the famous American sportsman). Many pathological cases at the cerebral level have been reported in boxing, also called, as a result of yet another distortion, the "noble art", but which has nothing neither noble nor artistic. It is a representative case of how the show's (cruel) needs, refusing a limitations through protective devices and the elimination of barbaric and anachronistic knock-out, force the professional sportsman to undergo additional risks compared to the amateur, who is authorized to protect his head.

7. The same protective devices are sometimes hazard indices of sports practices. Considering for example American football, a discipline as violent as is the capitalistic culture in which it is popular, the protections are even higher than those in the uniforms used in military missions. Nevertheless, it is now known that just like for the soldiers who operate in the vicinity of explosions, there is a correlation between this practice (together with the previously mentioned boxing, wrestling, hockey, and rugby) and degenerative disorders of the brain at a young age.

8. Today's sportive ideology exalts the search for sensational performance that finds its acme in the so-called extreme sports. These are particularly attractive to companies that want to advertise through the typical messages of the most irresponsible liberalism like "impossible is nothing" or "no limits". The human limitations (and the limitations of the slogans) do exist and manifest themselves sometimes dramatically, like for example when a famous ambassador unfortunately lost his life crashing during a flight of skydiving.

9. Sport is a predominantly male practice and the father of the modern sports-entertainment industry had misogynistic tendencies, which on several occasions until the last few years of life, thundered against the participation of women,[7] since women had to be limited to «crowning the winners».[8] Also for these reasons, with regard to the sexual sphere, the sportive environment

has always proved to be ambiguous, in which the woman was often relegated to ancillary, ornamental positions, the handsome assistant or crowner, a fascinating spectator caught by the cameras in the audience[9] almost always half-naked, less seriously in the role of an athlete and winner.[10] From the myth of virility to the taboo of homosexuality, through the sad events of intersex athletes, of humiliating inspections which for decades women have had to undergo in order to demonstrate that they are not men, of the sex schedule based on the matches up to the common "time castration"[11] represented by the practice of the "withdrawal" of athletes in locations distant from their families when they did not achieve the desired results.

10. On the level of the sports contribution towards the improvement of health, of great interest is the observation of Professor Fox:[12] «The problem is not that people do not go to the gym and do not practice sports [...] the problem is that we have stopped to be active in the general activities... collecting the leaves in the garden, doing the housework or climbing stairs are all good forms of moderate exercise. The key issue here, then, is not "What health benefits does sports guarantee?" But rather "What greater benefits for the health does sports guarantee compared to doing the housework?". In reality sports subtract public funds because of injuries».[13]

11. At the dawn of modern sport, the runners had to simulate horse racing (but without a horse, of course) by imitating the animal's movements, jumping fences and even giving themselves lashes on the legs. It was not an isolated case; the horse was so important that even in the races, bicycles, cars or boats also often had to recall the equine figure via some artifice.[14]

Back to running, the race conditions described appear ridiculous now. However, all those who competed were not crazy, they did it with seriousness and commitment similar to today's runners. They simply conformed to the sports model proposed to them without asking too many questions, just like they still do in sports.

12. The ideal of aesthetic perfection attributed to sports and dating back to the art of classical Greece and in particular in works such as the "Discobolus of Myron" could be faithful to the representation of athletes in certain disciplines of the time but it does not represent the athlete in its absolute sense, neither then (when other works, think of the "Resting Boxer by Lysippos"

highlighted the downfall), nor today. Except for a small number of sports, most of them negatively alter athletes' bodies, giving some imbalance, depending on the case.[15]

13. There is a primal instinctive behavior detectable over time and in multiple cultures, which consists of the voluntary deprivation of goods through gifts, or the destruction of these, in order to demonstrate wealth and generosity to then achieve glory, honor, or more important gifts. The ceremonies of this kind perpetrated by Native Americans - among which the phenomenon has been institutionalized and ritualized - have been called "Potlatch".

These are real competitions aimed at the victory and the hierarchical positioning, masked as altruism, generosity and friendship.

This atavistic impulse is particularly present in modern sports and even encouraged in its characterizing components, meaning the institutionalized competition and false solidarity represented by the hypocritical concept of fair play.

It therefore represents the perpetuation of a potlatch at international level, in which the athletes sacrifice their most precious possession - their own bodies - to achieve victory and the prestige that derives from it, implicitly challenging and forcing their rivals to do the same and to a greater extent.

NOTES

[1] JOE HUMPHREYS, *Foul Play: What's wrong with Sport* (London: Icon Books, 2008), 3.

[2] Practice consisting of dehydration adopted with the result of being less heavy in close competition where weight categories are planned, such as boxing, before recovering immediately afterwards and having heavier punches.

[3] JEAN-MARIE BROHM, *Sociologie politique du sport* (Nancy: Presses Universitaires de Nancy, 1992), 323. I ed. Paris: Éditions Universitaires, 1976.

[4] MARC PERELMAN, *Le sport Barbare. Critique d'un fléau mondial* (Paris: Michalon Éditions, 2008), 37.

[5] SANDRO PROVVISIONATO, *Lo sport in Italia. Analisi, storia, ideologia del fenomeno sportivo dal fascismo ad oggi* (Roma: Samonà e Savelli, 1978), 157.

[6] ROGER CAILLOIS, *I giochi e gli uomini. La maschera e le vertigine* (Milano: Bompiani, 1981). Orig. Les *jeux et les hommes. Le masque et le vertige.* Paris: Gallimard, 1958.

[7] Specifically, he wrote in "Les femmes aux Jeux olympiques", Revue olympique number 79 of July 1912 (109-111): «A small women's Olympic Games next to the large male Olympic Games. Where would the interest be? [...] Not practical, uninteresting, unaesthetic, and we are not afraid to add: incorrect, such would in our view this half female Olympics. It is not our conception of the Olympic games, in which we believe that we have tried and that we should continue to seek the realization of this formula: the solemn and periodic exaltation of male athleticism having internationalism as basis, loyalty as means, art as framework and female applause as reward».
Also in this case, it is not a historical rigor of a purist ancient athletic talking. In fact, precisely in the Olympia stadium *Heraia* ('Ηραῖα) were held, running races on foot for women, about as ancient as those for men.

[8] PIERRE DE FRÉDY DE COUBERTIN, *Pédagogie sportive* (Paris: Crés, 1922).

[9] CARLISLE DUNCAN, MARGARET, MICHAEL MESSNER, LINDA WILLIAMS, KERRY JENSEN, WAYNE WILSON. "Gender Stereotyping in Televised Sports", *The Amateur Athletic Foundation of Los Angeles*, (August 1990).

[10] The pinnacle of the global sports spectacle, the Olympic Games, are a good example of the role dedicated to women. From early Coubertin games of 1896, the first women's participation takes place only in 1928 in exchange for the renunciation of the "female Olympics" organized in 1921 by the French woman Milliat. The proportion of women and men will then be more heavily skewed toward the latter. Only men were members of the Olympic Committee until the eighties and even in these times, countries that do not guarantee women the right to practice sport are regularly admitted to the competitions.

[11] SANDRO PROVVISIONATO, op. cit., 156.

[12] Department of Exercise, Nutrition and Health Science, University of Bristol.

[13] JOE HUMPHREYS, op. cit., 20.

[14] GEORGES VIGARELLO, *Une histoire culturelle du sport* (Paris: Éditions Robert Laffont, 1988).

[15] MARC PERELMAN, op. cit., 39.

Sports and pacifism

1. That sports can be somewhat carriers of peace, is yet another myth that echoes in the propaganda by finding real foundation in the "Olympic Truce" that prevailed in ancient Greece. This never interrupted a war and the Greeks themselves, in fact, were never so unprepared to use a difficult word such as "peace" *(eirēnē)*, but *"ékecheiria"*, translated by circumlocution that defines a more realistic "situation where we abstain from using hands".[1] The truce, as Lämmer explains well, was not an ideal but an agreement [...] it did not cause any suspension of the war that was indeed an almost constant condition but ensured the organization of the contests "in spite of" the war.[2]

2. As noted by Heinila, «by its very nature, competitive sports does not seem particularly well suited to undertake the "dove of peace" function. The competition rewards few people, it frustrates many and, as a social process, in sociology is often classified under the chapter "social conflicts"».[3] In fact, many years ago Brohm denounced that «Far from leading to peace and brotherhood, sports exacerbate the chauvinism of the bell tower, nationalist passions. Far from procuring health and balance, sports push the tendency to self-destruction. In short, sports lead to the reversal of values».[4]

   Instead of making the real world known, these events spread trivial and counterproductive stereotypes about different countries. Each meeting is commented by newspapers and TV stations with the distinction between "us" and "them", in a typical logic (so-called of the Bedouin) for which "whoever is not with us is against us" or, in a more extensive formulation «my friend's friend is also my friend, the friend of my enemy is my enemy in turn, the enemy of my enemy is, as such, my friend, my enemy's friend is, in solidarity, my enemy».

   Inevitably, this accentuates the divisions and makes sports facilities the places chosen in which to vent aggression towards anyone who represents a geographic, ethnic, religious, or political diversity, or even more simply sporting a color different to ours.

3. It would certainly be simplistic to define the *Haka*, a typical dance of the Māori people known especially because it is carried out by some representative national rugby teams - in particular from New

Zealand - only as a war dance. Nevertheless it is, and the one staged in front of their opponents before each match, with all its typical components; the chorus screams that speak of life and death, eyes wide open, tongues hanging out of the mouth in defiance, the beating of hands on chest and thighs and the feet on the ground is meant to represent all the brutality and ferocity necessary to load the aggressiveness of their group and intimidate opponents.

4. Modern sports does not have the capacity nor the interest to make a contribution to the improvement of society; they assimilate, play and sometimes even amplify the problems.

5. It seems that the whole world has uncritically accepted the illusion of fairness towards the opponent in sport, while it is in fact the exception. Upon the occurrence of an event classified as "fair play" in fact, this makes the news, and it surprises the whole world, which stops to contemplate it. The sad normality is instead to acquire, lawfully or not, advantage over the opponent. Famous in this regard is the thought of Orwell, who said «Serious sport has nothing to do with fair play. It is bound up with hatred, jealousy, boastfulness, disregard of all rules and sadistic pleasure in witnessing violence: in other words it is war minus the shooting».[5] When in any competition there occurs couplings between sports groups representing entities who already have ongoing existing political conflicts or a more generic rivalry and hostility, no one rejoices thinking that thanks to that sporting event some divergence will be ironed out. On the contrary, it raises the alert and considerable law enforcement authorities are allocated in view of likely fights. This happens everywhere and at any level of competition up to those of worldwide importance, such as the aforementioned "Soccer War" between Honduras and El Salvador or that of hockey match between the Soviet Union and Czechoslovakia, both in 1969. [6] This is because the sports opposition is indeed a «moral equivalent of war»[7] and when it is not an occasion for fights, it is of boycotts, as happened in the Olympic Games of 1980 and 1984 by the United States, the Soviet Union and dozens of other countries who sided during the "cold war".

On the other hand, the so-called "friendly" matches (those played outside official competitions and aimed above all to maintain the workout, try changes and gather additional incomes) are usually considered the most boring ones just because they have a less aggressive component.

6. Even in the absence of further discord among the contenders, competitive sports teach them that the opponent has to be overcome because they are the obstacle that separates them from victory.

7. Institutionalized competitive sports require an extensive legal apparatus, the "sports justice" with its multiple bodies and its complex rules, which overlaps and often conflicts with the ordinary justice.

8. With the same uncritical attitude we accept that international competitions can make a contribution to global understanding and peace to the world. In such matches we often reach the point of learning the insults in the languages of the opponents to offend them more effectively.

It is certainly not by adding a field where to put the countries in contrast and encouraging the national chauvinism that you can think of achieving this goal. More effective would be the actual removal of barriers and an impetus towards mutual understanding.

9. In the wake of wanting to show what is not and to do the opposite of what it says, the international sporting government has historically given itself the role of "peacemaker", but when you contest it with the total absence of positive effects, it responds that its job is not the defense of human rights.

When - very rarely - the athletes come out from their role as gear of the spectacular machine to denounce social problems they are stigmatized, punished, deprived of achieved sports awards and finally marginalized. The intrinsic message for everyone else is that those who leave their part of sporting actor are immediately ejected from the system. In the wake of the old "hit one to educate a hundred".

Several large sponsor companies which usually finance the major events are involved in acts of war, environmental disasters, slave-labor conditions and anti-union activities.

The International Olympic Committee itself has not even given a signal whereas it could have had a practical effect, for example, by not lending itself at a worldwide legitimacy of dictatorial regimes by granting them the organization of competitions. Without having to go back to the examples of Nazism and of South

American military regimes, on the occasion of the much more recent games of Beijing 2008, the Olympic Committee endorsed the policies of a regime in which millions of women are eliminated at birth and others offered or purchased as goods, where thousands of executions still take place each year, where workers are abused and ethnic minorities or even political activists are persecuted.

One cannot but bitterly ascertain that further crimes are perpetrated precisely *because of* sporting events, on the occasion of which, and the resulting urban upheaval, all residents who are in the way of the cement project are brutally dispossessed and expelled.

These are just some of the reasons why any hint about the ideal of sports governing peace is laughable and hypocritical. Rightfully, the organization Reporters Without Borders has called the Olympic Committee «too cynical, too incompetent, or both things». For the same reason, the invented tradition of the Olympic torch around the world needs more and more outrageously police protection against the populations' anger towards what it represents.

10. While never claiming utopian ambitions of peace, the ancient Olympic Games lasted about twelve centuries without ever suffering a cancellation. In contrast, the modern Olympic Games of peace and brotherhood among peoples were suspended three times already in the first half century, precisely because of wars (1916, 1940 and 1944).[8]

11. Contrary to the fake do-gooders that ooze from the rhetoric of pacifism promoted by the Olympic Committee, its founder Coubertin (three times Nobel Peace Prize nominee) as well as other presidents, was a convinced militaristic. His whole project, in fact, is based on a nationalistic sentiment to strengthen France after the defeat against Prussia in 1870 and declared himself openly favorable to international rivalries of which Olympism was a carrier.

The perpetual association between the motto "the important thing is to participate" and later Coubertin, renders an image of a gentle and good-natured character that strides much with reality. It should be made clear in the meantime that the sentence went on to say: "The main thing is not to assert, but to fight well", to emphasize the taste for challenge and confrontation that, in truth, he never tried to hide but which in fact he claimed proudly. What remains of the ideal of sports as peacemaker is one of his brief articles[9] bearing this title, a speech on *"Pax olimpica"*[10], and really many unfulfilled good intentions.

Behind the ruling "the important thing is to participate", is instead concealed more faithfully the spirit of *"mors tua vita mea"*.

NOTES

[1] Manfred Lämmer in PAOLA ANGELI BERNARDINI (a cura di), *Lo sport in Grecia* (Roma / Bari: Laterza, 1998), 121.

[2] *Ibidem*, 139.

[3] Report to the international seminar CIEPS: *"Sport and International Understanding"*, Paris, 1971, in PIERRE SEURIN, *Problemi fondamentali dell'educazione fisica e dello sport* (Roma: Società Stampa Sportiva, 1981), 87. Orig. *Problèmes fondamentaux de l'éducation physique et du sport*. L'Union: Editions de la Violette, 1981.

[4] Jean-Marie Brohm in GIANNI BOCCARDELLI (a cura di), *I signori del gioco. Storia, massificazione, interpretazioni dello sport* (Napoli: Liguori editore, 1982), 23.

[5] GEORGE ORWELL, *The Sporting Spirit* (London: Tribune, 1945).

[6] RYSZARD KAPUŚCIŃSKI, *Wojna Futbolowa* (Warszawa: Czytelnik, 1978).

[7] William James in JIM PARRY, VASSIL GIRGINOV, *The Olympics. A Critical Reader* (New York / London: Routledge, 2008), 53.

[8] TONY PERROTTET, *The naked Olympics: The true story of the ancient games* (New York: Random House, 2004), 187.

[9] PIERRE DE FRÉDY DE COUBERTIN, *"Le sport est pacificateur"*, in La Revue sportive illustrée, XXXI, 1935, 44.

[10] Held in Germany in 1935.

Sports and benefit

1. Sports shows, quintessence of the dominant ideology, are everywhere at all times with such an intrusion that one might then wonder if another sport is possible. Since this is a tool and enactment of the power system, in the duality between cooperation and competition that is configured in human relationships, the latter has so far prevailed.

2. The worldwide sports organization is based on Coubertin's belief, that is however without any foundation, that «in order for one hundred to devote themselves to physical culture, it is necessary to have fifty who do sports; in order to have fifty who do sports, it is necessary that twenty specialize; in order for twenty to specialize, it is necessary that five are capable of amazing feats».[1] The sports show then, in the promise of benefits outside the usual, that they require extreme athlete specialization and promote a highly competitive spirit.

3. Even in ancient times Aristotle observed that athleticism as an end in itself does not produce benefits for either the civic life, nor for the health of the individual and, like Galen *(Claudius Galenus)*, he was in favor of milder practices directed toward the whole body.

4. Antagonism and competition between human beings, experienced all over this part of the sick world as a positive element, should never be anything other than an extreme conception of the social relationships, including sport.
   As questioned by Jacquard, «a society that offers to the youth the competition as the only moral life is a sick society».[2] This behavior, adds Caillat, would not be innate in the human being, as you might think, but rather a "cultural product", a social injunction culturally internalized.[3] The games, which mirror the society in which it is practiced, can be competitive or cooperative, depending on the rules of coexistence that a community takes on. There are indeed people (considered "inferior", in an ethnocentric and obtuse vision) devoid of competition such as the Inuit, in whose games the concept of victory is considered foolish, because the goals are enjoyment, balance and team play.
   There are non-competitive disciplines, such as the ancient Japanese *Kemari*, a cooperative game with a ball which provides neither winners nor losers. In such cooperative games you

challenge yourself to achieve a common goal and be comfortable together. The benefits are the creation and the harmony of a group, trust, respect, acceptance and mutual understanding as well as the self-esteem of the participants.

5. The "critical theory" positions could not be better described by what was done by Gutmann in his most famous book (who accused them) «What society needs is not greater pressure for more achievement, but freedom from the incessant demands for achievement [...] What society needs is not sports but play, not the "principle of reality" but the "principle of pleasure". Sport represses, play emancipates».[4]

   If the play is "the highest form of research",[5] one has to wonder whether it is correct to propose to the society and especially to young people a sport completely emptied of the recreational dimension. From the famous analysis of Huizinga,[6] it should be an established fact that the most significant feature of the play is that of being a free act.

6. For sports to return to the service of society, it is necessary first of all to regain at least "free" time, break free of the "victory" concept that is oppressive because it is absolute, in favor of a "success" in relation instead to oneself. And as claimed by Volpicelli, it would be essential to overturn the axiom of Coubertin that states that «for five to be capable of amazing feats it is necessary that twenty specialize. In order for twenty to specialize, fifty must do sports, a hundred people must turn to physical culture, the physical exercises and sports games of all sorts. It takes millions of sportive, then we will not have to carry out a sample research, they will come on their own».[7]

7. In order for the masses to learn about the alternatives, a radical social change would be required, where people regain possession basically of their own lives. When it becomes clear that the dominant model has been unsuccessful, it will be possible to develop a collective consciousness and there will be room for a more humane social system, where new approaches to sports can take shape, where this can make a contribution to the society, starting with really becoming a sport for all.

8. When we talk about sports we think of the great athletic feats, but in reality, no matter how sad, despite its name, most of the "records" are transitory and we forget them. With the passing of

years, nobody remembers who won most of the competitions, the trophies are covered with dust and the applauses fade into silence. For most people, in fact, sports are actually something much simpler: a run, a swim or a game among friends. What should really count is not so much the record, which temporarily belongs to only one individual and which remains inaccessible to the majority, but the personal records, realistic, small or large, to which everyone can aspire.

NOTES

[1] PIERRE DE FRÉDY DE COUBERTIN, *Pédagogie sportive* (Paris: Crés, 1922).

[2] Albert Jacquard in MICHEL CAILLAT, *Le sport* (Paris: Le Cavalier Bleu Éditions, 2008), 27.

[3] *Ibidem*, 28.

[4] ALLEN GUTTMANN, *Dal rituale al record. La natura degli sport moderni* (Napoli: Edizioni Scientifiche Italiane, 1994), 92. Orig. *From Ritual to Record: The Nature of Modern Sports*. New York: Columbia University Press, 1978.

[5] Neville V. Scarfe, attributed to Albert Einstein.

[6] JOHAN HUIZINGA, *Homo ludens. Proeve eener bepaling van het spel-element der cultuur* (Haarlem: H.D. Tjeenk Willink, 1938).

[7] LUIGI VOLPICELLI, *Industrialismo e sport (antisportivo)* (Roma: Armando Armando, 1960), 70.

Conclusions

Far from the happy haven of carefree, fun, cheerfulness, health, beauty and friendship that it seems, modern sports conceal the nature just described of a "free zone" in which they yield to a regression of human relationships to the law of the strongest, chauvinism and supremacy of gender and "race", and the exaltation of force as an end in itself. They awaken, call and exalt the baser instincts of human beings, in a sort of *"Bellum omnium contra omnes"*, the war of all against all theorized by Hobbes[1] or the sediment of a finely spread universal hatred which, according to Musil, plummets precisely in competitions. Reason, empathy, appreciation for diversity, and solidarity are all suspended during the times of organized sports.

This immoral background, notes Redeker,[2] is summed up in an exemplary way and unequivocally in the common wish of "May the strongest win!", or "May the best win!".

Although theoretically belonging to the sphere of free time, in modern sports - as "declination of the game in the capitalist way"[3] - all the negative values of an industrial society are projected, which tends towards the homogenization and flattening of the obsessive cycle of overproduction and overconsumption. In a context so empty and decaying, the collective irrationality manifests itself in competition both for production (looking for a job at any cost) and for consumption (purchase of goods to reach an increasingly higher social status). Even in sports we have therefore ended up with a preference towards the *quantity in* time rather than the *quality of* time, which is never enough because there are always more difficult *records* to break.

The new discovery of sports as a commodity to be sold in the form of a spectacle, combined with the discovery of its cultural anesthetic properties, has resulted in an increasing use of them, up to abusing them.

Alongside the deteriorating phenomena that proliferate around it, such as betting (defined as "sportive"), journalism reinforces its soothing effects. It does this on purpose, minimally taking care of the problems and making them appear as exceptions, content to live in the light reflected from champions and doing actually mere business communications on behalf of the companies involved, mixed with pure entertainment.

Thus, we are witnessing a phenomenon in which everything is somewhat shrill or exaggerated. The manifestations of happiness, for example, seem like uncontrollable neurotic attacks and the protagonists - only differently alienated from their audience - feel and act like pillars of humanity.

With the complicity of the international political class and local kleptocracies, the population is trapped in the only conception of sport, provided by what is, in fact, a private company.

Through the successes in this type of sport, many countries seek prestige at an international level, as if their victories in competitions were automatically synonymous with progress or superiority. However, it appears the opposite, even on a purely sporting level. For example the United States is largely first in the world in the Olympic successes, but - beyond the few top athletes - the US population does not excel in sports. The successes at the international level of the competitions evoke also a better well-being, yet in reality the USA have a notoriously suffering population, especially in terms of obesity and related illnesses. Prestige and superiority in international matches are not directly correlated to any possible political, social or cultural progress.

No real benefit is granted, not even such trumpeted peace among people. So much so that the sports historian Mandell defined instead some event as «a contribution to the international acrimony».[4] The rest is before the eyes of everyone and it is definitely not edifying; corruption, doping and the worst crimes that humanity can ever know, are sometimes carried out *in the name* of sports.

We are facing the biggest hoax in human history because it is perpetuated at all times and in all parts of the world throughout the year, and has been for many decades. Beyond it is taking place an ideological operation as well as a real fraud against the world's population. Who, in fact, if properly informed would agree to deprive their children of space, methods and times for a sport that would truly do them good, just so that some compatriots can go win, somewhere in the world, medals in disciplines such as shooting the carbine? It is not like this that we "celebrate the youth of the world" nor how we "inspire generations" to name a few slogans touting the modern sport.

Alongside the huge public investments that keep the gigantic organizational machine and its construction sites alive, significant parts of citizens residing in the same places live in poor conditions. The

Olympic Games of the centenary have ruined the public finances of Greece, simultaneously leaving abandoned sports facilities and children who no longer even go to the gym because they are debilitated due to the economic crisis.

So this is not a purely academic question, but true collective deprivation, deception and violence against society. If poverty is the worst form of violence[5] - as well as being the most widespread - this is somehow a war of some "institutions" against all the peoples. Today we look with horror to ancient Rome of *panem et circenses*, because the population was manipulated and, above all, slavery still existed. But we don't realize that today, the same thing is happening and many forms of "freely waged" work are far worse than the treatments that were reserved to the slaves in the past. Not always and not everyone, in fact, are able to grasp the barbarism that lies behind these concepts, now widely internalized and often accepted as the natural and unchangeable state of affairs. We all end up becoming, albeit of different sizes, small gears of the larger system.

That between those who seek to spread information and those who want to keep the underworld in sports is an uneven battle. On one hand there are few scholars who - with no particular livelihoods - are committed to make disclosure, also having to cope with the passage of time and the ordinary tasks of their life. In the past decades, many of these kind of lives have passed without seeing any changes. The "baton", to use a sports term, is passed on to other authors - even after many years - and is brought forward through new books which, such as this, update its documents and points of view but which yet, like the previous ones, must still face a powerful and wealthy scary machine.

This is represented by all sports organizations and policies which have a direct interest in perpetrating the hegemonic system and complacent sectors, those that have an indirect interest, such as the mass media.

It is not a painless process; those who have studied the matter end up having to join, often unconsciously, the system described. Who is writing this has chosen not to do so, preferring instead to stay out of it, in a kind of professional exile, as well as territorial.

We consider ourselves an evolved society only because we are pleasantly surprised by the technological innovations that surround us. But the inability to cooperate for the common good and the search for individual solutions against each other, the continued presence of wars, and anachronistic superstitions called religions create more trivial reasons of division, borders or even walls built to separate people are just a few specific examples to demonstrate the obtuse backwardness that permeates our time. We are unfortunately far from understanding that we are all inhabitants of this planet only for an infinitesimal fraction of its existence and that we should spend this short time to try to make our own good and that of others.

In sports, like in other areas of social life, it would be necessary to reverse the drift so far described, moving "the inertia of the righteous" and becoming collectively aware. In practical terms, taking back public affairs and participating actively in them, immediately ceasing any form of public funding both directly and indirectly to the "sports" show which - as such - is pleasant enough that it can still continue to support itself through its own income and resources. Finally, allocate and redistribute the funds released towards what is really needed in the community, including free spaces for basic sport, accessible anywhere, at any time.

But without a doubt, to paraphrase Feuerbach, our society still prefers to watch instead of taking action, illusion to disillusionment, spectacle to reality. What is sacred for it is only the appearance, and the peak of the sporting spectacle is also the peak of the mystification.

NOTES

[1] THOMAS HOBBES, *Leviathan, or The Matter, Forme and Power of a Common Wealth Ecclesiastical and Civil* (London: Andrew Crooke, 1651).

[2] ROBERT REDEKER, *Lo sport contro l'uomo* (Enna: Città Aperta, 2003), 61. Orig. *Le sport contre les peuples*. Paris: Berg International, 2002.

[3] ULRIKE PROKOP, *Olimpiadi dello spreco e dell'inganno* (Rimini: Guaraldi, 1972), 163. Orig. *Soziologie der Olympischen Spiele. Sport und Kapitalismus*. München: Carl Hanser, 1971.

[4] RICHARD MANDELL, *The First Modern Olympics* (Berkeley: University of California Press, 1976), 168.

[5] Attributed to Mohandās Karamchand Gāndhī.

Bibliography

Books

ALTOPIEDI, ROSALBA. *"Fatti" di sport. Il doping e la doppia morale delle organizzazioni sportive.* Milano: FrancoAngeli, 2009.

ANDERSON, BENEDICT, RICHARD O'GORMAN. *Imagined Communities: Reflections on the Origin and Spread of Nationalism.* London / New York: Verso, 1983.

ANGELI BERNARDINI, PAOLA (a cura di). *Lo sport in Grecia.* Roma / Bari: Laterza, 1998.

ANGELUCCI, MASSIMILIANO. *Il paradosso dello sport in Italia. Le scienze motorie e lo sport per tutti.* Frankfurt am Main: Biblioteca Italiana, 2015.

————. *La Responsabilità Sociale nello Sport.* Roma: Aracne, 2009.

————. *Tifo e appartenenza.* Napoli: Boopen, 2009.

————. *Tra fitness e wellness. Modelli di evento a confronto.* Milano: LdS, 2009.

BAUMAN, ZIGMUNT. *Liquid Modernity.* Cambridge / Malden: Polity Press, 2000.

BOCCARDELLI, GIANNI (a cura di). *I signori del gioco. Storia, massificazione, interpretazioni dello sport.* Napoli: Liguori editore, 1982.

BORTOLOTTI, ALESSANDRO. *Sport addio. Perché i giovani abbandonano la pratica sportiva.* Bari: La Meridiana, 2002.

BOSIO, ROBERTO. *I giochi del potere.* Cesena: Macro Edizioni, 2006.

BOUET, MICHEL. *Les motivations des sportifs.* Paris: Éditions Universitaires, 1969.

BROHM, JEAN-MARIE. *La Tyrannie sportive. Théorie critique d'un opium du peuple.* Paris: Beauchesne, 2006.

——————. *Sociologie politique du sport*. Nancy: Presses Universitaires de Nancy, 1992. I ed. Paris: Éditions Universitaires, 1976.

BROWNELL, SUSAN (edited by). *The 1904 Anthropology Days and Olympic Games: Sport, Race, and American Imperialism*. Lincoln / London: University of Nebraska Press, 2008.

BRUNAMONTINI, GIUSEPPE. *Esercito e Sport. Dal gesto individuale del guerriero mitologico all'educazione sportiva dei giovani di oggi*. Bari: Laterza, 1989.

BUCCIARELLI, CLAUDIO. *Lo sport come ideologia: alienazione o liberazione?* Roma: AVE, 1974.

CAILLAT, MICHEL. *Le sport*. Paris: Le Cavalier Bleu Éditions, 2008.

CAILLOIS, ROGER. *I giochi e gli uomini. La maschera e le vertigine*. Milano: Bompiani, 1981. Orig. *Les jeux et les hommes. Le masque et le vertige*. Paris: Gallimard, 1958.

CARCOPINO, JÉRÔME ERNEST JOSEPH, *La vita quotidiana a Roma all'apogeo dell'Impero*. Roma / Bari: Laterza, 1971. Orig. *La vie quotidienne à Rome à l'apogée de l'Empire*. Paris: Hachette, 1939.

DE FRÉDY, DE COUBERTIN PIERRE. *Mémoires olympiques*. Lausanne: Bureau International de Pédagogie Sportive, 1931.

——————. *Pédagogie sportive*. Paris: Crés, 1922.

——————. *Textes choisis*. Lausanne: Musée olympique, 1986.

DEBORD, GUY-ERNEST. *La societé du spectacle*. Paris: Éditions Buchet-Chastel, 1967.

DONATI, ALESSANDRO. *Campioni senza valore*. Firenze: Ponte alle Grazie, 1989.

——————. *Lo sport del doping. Chi lo subisce, chi lo combatte*. Torino: Edizioni Gruppo Abele, 2013.

FINLEY, MOSES ISRAEL, HENRI WILLY PLEKET. *I Giochi olimpici: I primi mille anni*. Roma: Editori Riuniti, 1980. Orig. *The Olympic Games: The First Thousand Years*. London: Chatto and Windus, 1976.

FRASCA, ROSELLA. *Religio Athletae. Pierre de Coubertin e la formazione dell'uomo per la società complessa.* Roma: Società Stampa Sportiva, 2007.

————. *Il corpo e la sua arte. Momenti e paradigmi di storia delle attività motorie, da Omero a P. de Coubertin.* Milano: Unicopli, 2006.

GIULIANOTTI, RICHARD (edited by). *Sport and Modern Social Theorists.* Basingstoke: Palgrave Macmillan, 2004.

GUTTMANN, ALLEN. *Dal rituale al record. La natura degli sport moderni.* Napoli: Edizioni Scientifiche Italiane, 1994. Orig. *From Ritual to Record: The Nature of Modern Sports.* New York: Columbia University Press, 1978.

HENSCHEN, HANS-HORST, REINHARD WETTER. *Anti-Olympia / Ein Beitrag zur mutwilligen Diffamierung und öffentlichen Destruktion der Olympischen Spiele und anderer Narreteien.* München: Carl Hanser Verlag, 1972.

HOBBES, THOMAS. *Leviathan, or the Matter, Forme and Power of a Common Wealth Ecclesiastical and Civil.* London: Andrew Crooke, 1651.

HOBERMAN, JOHN MILTON. *Politica e sport. Il corpo nelle ideologie politiche dell'800 e del 900.* Bologna: Il Mulino, 1988. Orig. *Sport and Political Ideology*, Austin: University of Texas Press, 1984.

HOBSBAWM ERIC J., TERENCE O. RANGER. *L'invenzione della tradizione.* Torino: Einaudi, 1987. Orig. *The Invention of Tradition.* Cambridge / New York: Cambridge University Press, 1983.

HUIZINGA, JOHAN. *Homo ludens.* Torino: Einaudi, 1949. Orig. *Homo ludens. Proeve eener bepaling van het spel-element der cultuur.* Haarlem: H.D. Tjeenk Willink, 1938.

HUMPHREYS, JOE. *Foul Play: What's wrong with Sport.* London: Icon Books, 2008.

INTERNATIONAL OLYMPIC COMMITTEE. *Olympic Charter.* Lausanne, 2011.

INTERNATIONAL OLYMPIC COMMITTEE. *Olympic Marketing Fact File.* Lausanne, 2015.

136

IRLINGER, PAUL, CATHERINE LOUVEAU, MICHÈLE MÉTOUDI. *Les pratiques sportives des Français*. Paris: INSEP, 1987.

JENNINGS, ANDREW. *The New Lord of the Rings. Olympic Corruption and How to Buy Gold Medals*. London: Transparency Books, 2012.

KAPUŚCIŃSKI, RYSZARD. *La prima guerra del football e altre guerre di poveri*. Milano: Serra e Riva, 1990. Orig. *Wojna Futbolowa*. Warszawa: Czytelnik, 1978.

LAGUILLAUMIE, PIERRE. *Sport & repressione*. Roma: Samonà e Savelli, 1971. Orig. *Sport, culture et répression*. Paris: Maspero, 1968.

MANDELL, RICHARD D. *The First Modern Olympics*, University of California Press. Berkeley, 1976.

MITCHELL, DAVID STEPHEN. *Cloud Atlas*. London: Sceptre, 2004.

MORRIS, DESMOND JOHN. *The Soccer Tribe*. London: Jonathan Cape, 1981.

ORWELL, GEORGE. *Nineteen Eighty-Four*. London: Secker & Warburg, 1949.

PARRY, JIM, VASSIL GIRGINOV. *The Olympics. A Critical Reader*. New York / London: Routledge, 2008.

PERELMAN, MARC. *Sport barbaro. Critica di un flagello mondiale*. Milano: Medusa, 2012. Orig. *Le sport Barbare. Critique d'un fléau mondial*. Paris: Michalon Éditions, 2008.

PERROTTET, TONY. *The naked Olympics: The true story of the ancient games*. New York: Random House, 2004.

PORRO, NICOLA. *Sociologia del calcio*. Roma: Carocci, 2008.

PROKOP, ULRIKE. *Olimpiadi dello spreco e dell'inganno*. Rimini: Guaraldi, 1972. Orig. *Soziologie der Olympischen Spiele. Sport und Kapitalismus*. München: Carl Hanser, 1971.

PROVVISIONATO, SANDRO. *Lo sport in Italia. Analisi, storia, ideologia del fenomeno sportivo dal fascismo ad oggi*. Roma: Samonà e Savelli, 1978.

REDEKER, ROBERT. *Lo sport contro l'uomo*. Enna: Città Aperta, 2003. Orig. *Le sport contre les peuples*. Paris: Berg International, 2002.

RIGAUER, BERO. *Sport and Work*. New York: Columbia University Press, 1981. Orig. *Sport und Arbeit*. Frankfurt am Main: Suhrkamp, 1969.

RIVA, GIGI. *L'ultimo rigore di Faruk. Una storia di calcio e di guerra*. Palermo: Sellerio, 2016.

SEURIN, PIERRE. *Problemi fondamentali dell'educazione fisica e dello sport*. Roma: Società Stampa Sportiva, 1981. Orig. *Problèmes fondamentaux de l'éducation physique et du sport*. L'Union: Editions de la Violette, 1981.

TOMLINSON, ALAN, GARRY WHANNEL. *Five-ring Circus: Money, Power and Politics at the Olympic Games*. London: Pluto Press, 1984.

TURANO, GIANFRANCESCO. *Fuori gioco. Calcio e potere. Da Della Valle a Berlusconi, da Preziosi a Moratti. La vera storia dei presidenti di Serie A*. Milano: Chiarelettere, 2012.

TUTKO, THOMAS A., BILL BRUNS. *Winning is Everything and Other American Myths*. New York: MacMillan, 1976.

VALERI, MAURO. *Stare ai giochi. Olimpiadi tra discriminazioni e inclusioni*. Roma: Odradek Edizioni, 2012.

VIGARELLO, GEORGES. *Culture e tecniche dello sport. Gesti, strumenti, materiali, organizzazioni: un'antropologia dei fenomeni sportivi nella società contemporanea*. Milano: il Saggiatore, 1993. Orig. *Une histoire culturelle du sport*. Paris: Éditions Robert Laffont, 1988.

VILLEPREUX, OLIVIER. *Feue la flamme. Pour en finir avec les JO*. Paris: Gallimard, 2008.

VINNAI, GERHARD. *Il calcio come ideologia. Sport e alienazione nel mondo capitalista*. Rimini: Guaraldi, 2004. Orig. *Fußballsport als Ideologie*. Frankfurt am Main: Europäische Verlagsanstalt, 1970.

VON CLAUSEWITZ, CARL PHILIPP GOTTLIEB. *Vom Kriege: Hinterlassenes Werk des Generals Carl von Clausewitz*. Berlin: Dümmler, 1832.

VOLPICELLI, LUIGI. *Industrialismo e sport (antisportivo)*. Roma: Armando Armando, 1960.

WANN DANIEL L., MERRILL J. MELNICK, GORDON W.RUSSELL, DALE G. PEASE. *Sport fans: The psychology and social impact of spectators*. New York / London: Routledge, 2001.

WEEBER, KARL-WILHELM. *Olimpia e i suoi sponsor. Sport, denaro e politica nell'antichità.* Milano: Garzanti, 1992. Orig. *Die unheiligen Spiele. Das antike Olympia zwischen Legende und Wirklichkeit.* Zürich / München: Artemis Verlag, 1991.

————. *Panem et circenses. La politica dei divertimenti di massa nell'antica Roma.* Milano: Garzanti, 1989. Orig. *Panem et circenses.* Düsseldorf / Wien: Econ Verlag, 1983.

YOUNG, DAVID C. *The Modern Olympics. A Struggle for Revival.* Baltimore / London: Johns Hopkins University Press, 1996.

————. *The Olympic Myth of Greek Amateur Athletics.* Chicago: Ares Publishers, 1984.

Others

CALLEBAT, LOUIS. "The Modern Olympic Games and their Model in Antiquity". *Boston University - Third Meeting of the International Society for the Classical Tradition*, (March 1995).

CARLISLE DUNCAN, MARGARET, MICHAEL MESSNER, LINDA WILLIAMS, KERRY JENSEN, WAYNE WILSON. "Gender Stereotyping in Televised Sports", *The Amateur Athletic Foundation of Los Angeles*, (August 1990).

COMITÉ INTERNATIONAL OLYMPIQUE. *Bulletin.* Lausanne, (15 Février 1965).

CONSIGLIO D'EUROPA. "Carta Europea dello Sport", Consiglio d'Europa, Rodi, (1992).

DE FRÉDY, DE COUBERTIN PIERRE. "L'Éducation de la paix", *La Réforme Sociale*, 2 série, tome VII, (16 Septembre 1889).

DE FRÉDY, DE COUBERTIN PIERRE. "Le sport est pacificateur", *La Revue sportive illustrée*, XXXI, (1935).

DE FRÉDY, DE COUBERTIN PIERRE. "Les femmes aux Jeux olympiques", *Revue olympique,* n.79 (juillet 1912).

EUROPEAN TOUR OPERATORS ASSOCIATION. "Olympic Report", London, (2012).

ORTEGA Y GASSET, JOSÉ. "El origen deportivo del Estado" (1924), *Obras Completas*, Vol. II, Ed. Taurus, Madrid (1963).

ORWELL GEORGE. "The Sporting Spirit", London, Tribune, (1945).

TURRINI, DAVIDE. "Silvano Agosti: Il cinema è in agonia e gli spettatori mi fanno una pena infinita", *Il Fatto Quotidiano*, (7 luglio 2016).

VENDEMIALE, LORENZO. "Olanda, in tv documentario sul doping nella Juve anni '90 (con troppe omissioni)", *Il Fatto Quotidiano*, (28 maggio 2013).

YOUNG, DAVID C. "Further Thoughts on Some Issues of Early Olympic History", *Journal of Olympic History*, Volume 6 n.3 (Fall 1998).